# THE
# WOK BIBLE

BY
## YANG HONG

# TABLE OF CONTENTS

**INTRODUCTION** ........................................................................................................ vii

**CHAPTER 1: ASIAN CUISINE HISTORY** ............................................................ 1

**CHAPTER 2: HISTORY OF WOK** ......................................................................... 2

WHAT IS A WOK? ..................................................................................................... 2

An In-Depth History of The Wok .......................................................................... 2

WHAT ARE WOKS MADE OF? ............................................................................. 3

BENEFITS ..................................................................................................................... 4

HOW TO SEASON AND CLEAN A WOK ........................................................... 4

**CHAPTER 3: POPULAR COOKING METHODS FOR ASIAN CUISINE** ...... 8

THESE ARE THE TOP ASIAN COOKING TECHNIQUES ................................ 8

**CHAPTER 4: PAN ASIAN RECIPES** .................................................................... 10

JAPAN ......................................................................................................................... 10

    1. ZOSUI (JAPANESE RICE SOUP) .................................................................. 10

    2. YAKI UDON (JAPANESE STIR-FRIED UDON NOODLES) ................... 11

    3. TOSHIKOSHI SOBA (NEW YEAR'S EVE SOBA NOODLE SOUP) ....... 13

    4. EASY JAPANESE FRIED RICE (YAKIMESHI) .......................................... 15

    5. GYUDON (JAPANESE BEEF RICE BOWL) .............................................. 17

    6. OYAKODON (CHICKEN AND EGG RICE BOWL) ................................ 18

    7. TERIYAKI TOFU ............................................................................................. 21

    8. TAMAGOYAKI (JAPANESE ROLLED OMELETTE) ............................... 22

    9. JAPANESE EGG SANDWICH (TAMAGO SANDO) ............................... 24

    10. MISO BUTTER PASTA WITH TUNA AND CABBAGE ......................... 25

    11. NAPOLITAN (JAPANESE KETCHUP SPAGHETTI) ............................. 27

    12. VEGETARIAN RAMEN ................................................................................ 29

    13. MISO RAMEN ................................................................................................ 31

    14. BEEF UDON ................................................................................................... 32

    15. MISO SALMON .............................................................................................. 35

    16. TERIYAKI SALMON ...................................................................................... 36

    17. VEGGIE YAKI UDON ................................................................................... 38

    18. CHICKEN TERIYAKI .................................................................................... 39

19. AGEDASHI TOFU .................................................................................................... 41

20. CURRY UDON ...................................................................................................... 42

CHINA ........................................................................................................................... 44

1. SINGAPORE NOODLES WITH PRAWNS ........................................................ 44

2. HEALTHY CHICKEN STIR-FRY ...................................................................... 45

3. CRISPY CHILI BEEF ........................................................................................ 46

4. STEAMED SEA BASS WITH BLACK BEAN SAUCE ...................................... 47

5. PORK & CRAB 'ANTS CLIMBING TREES' ..................................................... 48

6. CROSSING THE BRIDGE NOODLES ............................................................. 49

7. PRAWNS IN LONGJING TEA ......................................................................... 50

8. SALT AND PEPPER CHICKEN ....................................................................... 51

9. STEAMED BASS WITH GARLIC & CHILI ...................................................... 52

10. SWEET & SOUR TOFU .................................................................................. 53

11. KUNG PAO CAULIFLOWER & PRAWN STIR-FRY ...................................... 54

12. CHINESE-STYLE KALE ................................................................................. 55

13. CRISPY DUCK PANCAKES ........................................................................... 55

14. CHINESE CHICKEN NOODLE SOUP WITH PEANUT SAUCE ..................... 57

15. QUICK & EASY HOT-AND-SOUR CHICKEN NOODLE SOUP ..................... 58

16. MARINATED TOFU WITH PAK CHOI ........................................................... 59

17. VEGGIE CHINESE PANCAKES ..................................................................... 60

18. CHINESE SPICED DUCK SALAD .................................................................. 61

19. HONEY & SOY DUCK SALAD ....................................................................... 62

20. CRISPY CHILI BEEF ...................................................................................... 63

THAI ............................................................................................................................. 64

1. TOM YUM SOUP WITH PRAWNS .................................................................. 64

2. THAI CHICKEN AND SWEET POTATO SOUP ............................................... 65

3. AUTHENTIC PAD THAI .................................................................................. 66

4. THAI-STYLE STEAMED FISH ......................................................................... 67

5. RED CURRY CHICKEN KEBABS .................................................................... 68

6. THAI PRAWN, GINGER & SPRING ONION STIR-FRY .................................. 68

7. LEMONGRASS BEEF STEW WITH NOODLES .............................................. 69

8. THAI CHICKEN CAKES WITH SWEET CHILI SAUCE ................................... 70

9. THAI-STYLE FISH BROTH WITH GREENS .................................................... 71

10. TILAPIA IN THAI SAUCE .............................................................................. 72

11. THAI PRAWNS WITH PINEAPPLE & GREEN BEANS .................................. 73

12. THAI MUSSELS & PRAWNS .......................................................................... 74

13. THAI GREEN CURRY ..................................................................................... 75

iv

14. EASY PAD THAI ............................................................................................................76

15. THAI BEEF WITH COCONUT DRESSING ..................................................................77

16. 10-MINUTE PAD THAI ...............................................................................................78

17. FRESH SALMON WITH THAI NOODLE SALAD ........................................................79

18. LEFTOVER ROAST CHICKEN PAD THAI ..................................................................80

19. PRAWN & COCONUT SOUP .....................................................................................81

20. THAI BEEF SALAD .....................................................................................................82

INDIA ......................................................................................................................................83

1. BOMBAY POTATO FISHCAKES ................................................................................83

2. SQUASH & CABBAGE SABZI .....................................................................................84

3. GOAN PRAWN & COCONUT CURRY WITH CUMIN RICE .....................................85

4. INDIAN-SPICED FISH CAKES ...................................................................................86

5. SWEET & SOUR LENTIL DHAL WITH GRILLED AUBERGINE ...............................87

6. CURRY COCONUT FISH PARCELS ...........................................................................88

7. TANDOORI SPICED SEA BREAM ..............................................................................89

8. INDIAN LAMB CUTLETS ...........................................................................................90

9. SAMOSA CHAAT ........................................................................................................90

10. EGG CURRY ...............................................................................................................91

11. WEST INDIAN SPICED AUBERGINE CURRY ..........................................................92

12. INDIAN CHICKPEAS WITH POACHED EGGS .........................................................93

13. INDIAN SWEET POTATO & DHAL PIES ..................................................................94

14. SOUTH INDIAN COCONUT & PRAWN CURRY .....................................................95

15. CHICKEN SATAY SALAD ..........................................................................................96

16. SOUTH INDIAN COCONUT & PRAWN CURRY .....................................................97

17. MATAR PANEER ........................................................................................................98

18. LENTIL & SWEET POTATO CURRY .........................................................................99

19. SOUTH INDIAN FISH CURRY WITH CHICKPEAS ................................................100

20. PRAWN CURRY IN A HURRY .................................................................................101

KOREAN ...............................................................................................................................102

1. SPICY KIMCHI PANCAKE (KIMCHI JEON) ............................................................102

2. STIR-FRIED KOREAN BEEF .....................................................................................103

3. EASY BIBIMBAP .......................................................................................................104

4. JAPCHAE (STIR FRIED NOODLES) .........................................................................105

5. KOREAN-STYLE PRAWN & SPRING ONION PANCAKE ........................................106

6. KOREAN SESAME PORK STIR-FRY .........................................................................107

7. TORNADO OMELETTE .............................................................................................108

8. BULGOGI ..................................................................................................................109

9. BEAN & HALLOUMI STEW ...................................................................................................110

10. LIVER AND ONIONS .......................................................................................................111

11. CREAMY SALMON, LEEK & POTATO TRAYBAKE ............................................................111

12. TOFU SCRAMBLE ...........................................................................................................112

13. BEST-EVER GAZPACHO ..................................................................................................113

14. CHICKEN NOODLE SOUP ...............................................................................................114

15. KOREAN FRIED CHICKEN ..............................................................................................115

16. KOREAN-STYLE FRIED RICE ..........................................................................................116

17. KOREAN FISHCAKES WITH FRIED EGGS & SPICY SALSA .............................................117

18. CELERY SOUP ...............................................................................................................118

19. MUSHROOM STROGANOFF ............................................................................................119

20. KOREAN FRIED RICE .....................................................................................................120

# INTRODUCTION

Pan Asian recipes are derived from countries that use simple-to-cook sprouts and leafy vegetables together with various herbs and aromatic spices, including kaffir lime leaves, mint, basil, and coriander. These are commonly found in local street markets and are widely used in Thai, Chinese, Malaysian, Vietnamese, and Cambodian cuisines.

They also use other ingredients like raw papaya, cabbage, broccoli, bok choi, ginger, garlic, coconut, onion, turmeric, fresh chilies, galangal, sesame, and ginseng in most of their dishes, especially in slow-cooked hotpots, stews, and stir-fries. Asian food is very popular all around the world. The cuisine offers a mix of flavors in its numerous dishes.

If Pan-Asian is your favorite cuisine and you're seeking cooking ideas for your kitchen, you are reading the right book. Explore the many Asian cuisines, which are all known for their exceptional flavors and beautiful colors. Ingredients common to many cultures of the region include ginger, rice, garlic, chilies, sesame seeds, and soy; steaming, deep-frying, and stir-frying are the most popular cooking techniques used to make mouthwatering dishes. And the rich curries that make pan-Asian cuisine such a global vogue are made with coconut milk, which is an excellent way to bring out the flavors.

There is much more than sushi to choose from regarding Japanese food. There are numerous contrasting textures in play, ranging from silken tofu to crispy tempura, which helps you savor the mild, simple flavors and heightens the experience.

Did you know that rice plays a vital role in pan-Asian cuisine? Asides sushi is also used in Japan to make sake, a well-known alcoholic beverage. Rice is the foundation of practically every dish in Korean and Thai cuisines.

Does Korean food begin and end at kimchi for you? While it is a vital component of their meals, Korean cuisine emphasizes artistic presentation and strong, hot flavors. It focuses on spices, seafood, and sides (banchan). Sesame oil, chili pepper paste, soy sauce, and scallions are among the most popular Korean spices.

Regarding Pan Asian cuisine, Chinese food, arguably the most favored, uniquely blends flavors in many ways. Make your own at home, from stir-fries to sizzling sea bass. The cooking technique of steaming is ideal for those trying to consume fewer calories. Sichuan cuisine is spicy, Shandong is often crispy and tangy, and Cantonese food is sweet. Chinese food truly differs a lot from region to region. Try rustling them up at home if you are craving scrumptious dumplings or kung pao chicken.

Thai cuisine balances bold flavors; imagine creamy curries and exotic notes created by combining aromatic ingredients like kaffir lime leaves, lemon grass, galangal, shallots, and fish sauce. Every meal, from the simple Som Tum papaya salad to Pad Thai, is a gastronomic treat. The roots of Malay and Indonesian cuisines are also founded on the art of harmonizing flavors. How can you forget about dishes like Nasi Goreng, Rendang, nourishing Laksa, and others? And now that so many specialty stores sell these products, it's not hard to recreate these dishes in your home.

Vietnamese is one of the lesser-known cuisines, and it screams simplicity. Local fresh vegetables are cooked in flavorful stocks. The most popular dish worldwide is Pho, a noodle soup, followed by rice paper rolls. On the other hand, Thai food and Cambodian cuisine are highly similar, emphasizing bold flavors and rich curries produced with coconut milk. One of their favorite foods is amok, a delicious curry cooked with either fish or chicken. Furthermore, Cambodians are renowned for their whole fish dishes, like sizzling red snapper curry with pineapples.

# CHAPTER 1

# ASIAN CUISINE HISTORY

There are many kinds of food worldwide, including Asian cuisine. Asian cooking is one of the most popular cuisines in the world for various reasons. Every Asian cuisine is prepared differently and has distinctive flavors that impact people. In Queenscliff, there is already an Asian restaurant serving the best selection of Asian cuisine. There is no denying this specific cuisine's appeal. But what exactly is Asian cooking, and why is it so popular worldwide? Here are the things that you need to know.

Asian cooking originated in 3000 B.C. when the earliest agriculture was discovered alongside one of the major Asian and Indian civilizations. Because the Europeans colonized various nations in the southeast, there have historically been indications of European influence in Asian cuisine. Nevertheless, over time, several types of Asian cuisine have emerged. The Persian-Arabian civilization's unique cooking technique is featured in the southwest style.

Curry, rice, and chapatti are common meals in India, Pakistan, Sri Lanka, and Burma. In the northeast, fats, oils, and sauces were used in large quantities during cooking. Despite being widely consumed, Chinese cuisine has surpassed Japanese and Korean cuisine in popularity. While the skill of stir-frying and steaming employing unique citrus herbs and spices is popular in the southeast, encompassing cuisines from Thailand, Vietnam, Indonesia, Laos, Cambodia, Malaysia, Brunei, and Singapore. Asian cuisine has a rich history that is reflected in its dishes. And at the moment, every restaurant serving Asian food has gradually popped up worldwide, enriching and developing this specific cooking method.

# CHAPTER 2

# HISTORY OF WOK

W e thought we'd take a deeper look at the wok's history with our fun facts about the history of a wok. Wok is an essential part of Asian cuisine, as we are all aware. The wok's origins and how it became such a widely used culinary utensil around the globe will be covered in this section.

## WHAT IS A WOK?

A wok is a cooking utensil with a round bottom, and high edges, typically with two side handles or one larger handle. Food cooks faster in a wok because heat is spread more uniformly than in a saucepan due to the wok's rounded bottom. When cooking a stir fry, the high walls make it easier for food to be tossed, allowing the ingredients to combine and cook evenly.

## An In-Depth History of The Wok

### Where Was the Wok Invented?

The wok is thought to have been created for the first time in China over 2000 years ago, during the Han dynasty. Early versions of the wok, which is Cantonese for "cooking pot," were made of cast iron metals, which made them more lasting and durable.

### What Was the Wok First Used For?

The origins of the wok are the subject of numerous ideas from historians and chefs. Some claim that the wok's versatility enabled a variety of meals to be prepared using the same ingredients during the shortage of food back in the Han dynasty.

Another theory holds that because tribes had to take all of their possessions with them when they traveled across the country in the past, they required a cooking tool that was both portable and fast to prepare large quantities of food.

Another theory is that the wok enabled people to prepare food with very little oil during the Han period due to a lack of fuel and oil. You may have already observed that using a wok at home to prepare your ingredients only requires a small quantity of vegetable oil!

## The Modern Wok

Nowadays, a wide variety of dishes are prepared in the wok all over the globe. Most woks are made of carbon steel, making them lightweight to take up while still being strong and non-stick.

The wok is indispensable when preparing Asian cuisine but has many other applications. One of the world's most adaptable culinary utensils, the wok can be used for various cooking methods, including:

- Stir-frying
- Pan-frying
- Deep frying
- Steaming
- Boiling
- Smoking
- Stewing
- Braising
- Searing

Because of the design, heat can be spread equally throughout the entire wok, ensuring that all ingredients cook and are ready simultaneously. Furthermore, a huge advantage of using a wok is that you can prepare it with little oil and still have delicious, non-stick food. Sometimes you'll also need wok accessories, like a wok lid for steaming or boiling or even a wok ring to keep your wok from sliding around while cooking.

## WHAT ARE WOKS MADE OF?

Each wok material has unique qualities and advantages. From the non-stick perk of properly seasoned carbon steel or cast iron woks to the non-porous nature of stainless steel. Before making a purchase, it's important to know the highlights of each material.

## Carbon Steel Woks

Carbon steel is one of the most widely used materials for woks. Many chefs in the industry prefer it because of its durability and ability to heat food quickly and evenly. An experienced chef can easily lower the chance of food sticking to the pan with the right seasoning. Carbon steel pans can also be used with wok induction ranges because they are magnetic.

3

## Stainless Steel Woks

Stainless steel is a very durable material with a polished appearance. It doesn't require as much seasoning as cast iron or carbon steel to perform at its best because it is less porous. It is also easy to clean due to its surface's natural smoothness.

## Cast Iron Woks

Compared to other cookware materials, cast iron is more durable and can retain heat for a longer period, saving energy. It becomes more seasoned as it is used, increasing its non-stick qualities as it ages rather than losing them.

## BENEFITS

## Healthy

Wok cooking has the benefit of using less oil than other frying techniques, making it a healthy option. Additionally, food can be moved along the edges to allow extra oil to drip off before serving.

## Effective and efficient

The wok is energy-efficient and excellent for cooking. Less energy is used because of its high heat-holding capacity, and continuously stirring while frying speeds up the heating process. Carbon steel heats evenly, but a wok has two different cooking 'zones.' Food is seared at the bottom where the heat source is, while higher up, food is steam cooked. It is partly because with constant stirring, the food is being steamed and fried simultaneously, which speeds up the cooking process and results in an ideal result.

Another advantage of using a wok when cooking is that it's easy to move food around the surface without spilling it over the edges due to its elevated, sloping walls.

## Versatile

However, the wok is a very useful tool that can be used for more than just stir-frying. In eastern Asia, woks have traditionally been used for every cooking type, including braising, deep frying, boiling, pan frying, searing, smoking, roasting, stewing, steaming, and stir-frying.

## Durable

Woks are incredibly durable. Carbon steel will rust, so it needs to be seasoned, which isn't difficult. The seasoning is made up of layers of polymerized veggie oil, which prevents the wok from corrosion and makes it relatively non-stick and easier to clean. A well-maintained wok could easily last a lifetime.

## HOW TO SEASON AND CLEAN A WOK

After choosing the type of wok that suits you the best, it's time to decide whether it needs to be seasoned. Porous metal woks like carbon steel and cast iron must be seasoned to avoid corrosion. You can follow the step-by-step directions to properly clean, season, and care for your new cookware.

## How to Season a Wok

Every chef has a preferred technique for seasoning their pans. Three of the most common techniques will be covered: salt seasoning, oven seasoning, and stovetop seasoning. Regardless of the seasoning technique, washing the wok to expose the bare metal is always the first step.

## How to Season a Wok on a Stovetop

The stovetop technique is a common way to season your wok. You will need a range top burner, paper towels, and the oil of your choice.

- If your wok has wooden handles, remove or cover them in aluminum foil to avoid scorching/burning.
- Preheat the wok over high heat to allow the metal's pores to open. Ensure the area around your stove is free of obstructions, your kitchen hood fan is on, and your windows are open because the wok will become extremely heated and emit smoke.
- Tilt and flip your wok to heat the back, front, and sides. The heat will cause your wok to change colors.
- Throw a drop of water on the pan to test the water. If your wok is heated enough, the water will immediately evaporate, indicating it is ready for seasoning.
- Let the wok cool until it is safe to touch.
- Apply high smoke point oil to your wok using a paper towel. To obtain a smooth, nonstick surface, maintain the oil layer as even and sparse as possible. Ensure you oil the outside of your wok because seasoning also serves as a corrosion preventative.
- Return your wok to the burner over medium heat. Once the oil stops smoking, that area of the wok is seasoned. To season each section, continue to flip and tilt the wok.
- The seasoning procedure is complete when the entire surface of your wok has turned matte and black.
- To clean the wok without removing the seasoning, rinse it with hot water and scrub it with a bamboo wok brush.
- Return the wok to your burner and heat it to a high heat to burn off any residual water droplets.
- Re-season the wok if necessary or keep it until you can use it. Season the wok up to three times for a smoother nonstick surface and a thicker protective covering.

## How to Season a Wok in the Oven

This technique recommends for woks with oven-safe handles.

- Set the oven's temperature to 450 degrees Fahrenheit.
- Use aluminum foil to line a sheet pan.
- The outside of the pan should also be coated with lard, shortening, or oil using a paper towel.
- Put the lined sheet pan on the oven's bottom rack.
- Put the oiled wok on the highest rack.
- After 20 minutes of baking, take the pan out of the oven.
- Use a soft sponge and warm water to rinse the wok.
- Dry it thoroughly on the stovetop over high heat.

## How to Season a Wok with Salt

- Chop veggies on a cutting board over a wok.
- Use Kosher salt to give your wok a dark patina. A wok that hasn't been used in a while can also be revived or re-seasoned.
- Add 1 cup of kosher salt to a wok.
- Place the wok, filled with salt, on a gas stovetop and turn the heat to high.
- Stir salt continuously for twenty minutes, pushing the salt up and around the sides of the wok.
- Remove the wok from the heat after 20 minutes, then pour the heated salt into the sink (allowing it cool before you discard it).
- Spread some oil on the wok's surface and use an oil-covered cloth or paper towel to clean it.

## Why Season a Wok?

Seasoning your carbon steel or cast-iron wok creates a patina. A well-seasoned wok will have a smooth non-stick surface and help infuse flavors into the dishes prepared inside. Any food cooked in your wok without seasoning it first will likely stick and lack flavor.

## What Is a Patina?

This is a protective coating inside the wok. The coating improves the taste of the food prepared in your wok while preventing corrosion and rust. When you cook with oil in your wok, the patina gets denser and thicker, forming a naturally non-stick surface.

- Cook, saute, and frequently fry to continuously build a patina
- Invest in a wok ladle, wok spatula, and bamboo wok brush.
- Avoid steaming, boiling, or poaching products in your new wok.
- Do not cook with acidic products in a newly seasoned wok, including vinegar, lemon, and tomatoes.
- Avoid using abrasive pads or any ware washing chemicals, including sanitizers and soaps.

## How to Clean a Wok

The first thing you should do after buying a new wok is to sanitize it. Manufacturers apply factory oil to fresh woks to prevent moisture damage during shipping. By doing this, rust is avoided, and the wok is delivered in perfect condition.

You must thoroughly clean your new wok with a sponge and detergent to eliminate all the factory grease and any shipping-related dust before you can season it. After this, you won't need to scrub your pan with soap and an abrasive sponge again. Follow these instructions to get rid of all residues:

- Fill a sink with hot, soapy water.
- Scrub the interior and exterior of wok with a scouring pad.
- Rinse the wok thoroughly.
- Use a clean, dry towel to dry wok.
- Place the wok on a stovetop and heat it to medium-high to fully dry it and evaporate any remaining water.

## How to Clean a Wok After Use

The maintenance guidelines that came with your wok should always be followed. Normally, woks made of metal, stainless steel, or copper can be placed in the dishwasher. Woks made of carbon steel or cast iron must be handled carefully to prevent the flavor from being lost during cleaning. After cooking, simply follow these steps:

- Rinse wok in warm or hot water.
- You can submerge it in pure boiling water free of soap or chemicals if you need to sanitize it to comply with specific regulations.
- Use a sponge or wok brush to carefully scrub away any food particles.
- Don't use abrasive scouring pads, sanitizers, ware washing chemicals, or soaps as they'll remove the seasoned surface you just created.
- Remove any loosened particles by rinsing.
- Dry completely with a towel.
- Place the wok over a medium-high heat source to complete the drying and evaporation of residual moisture.
- We advise adding a thin coating of oil or lard to your wok if you intend to keep it for longer than a week without using it to further preserve the patina.

## How to Clean a Wok with Rust

To simplify rust removal, you must first soak your wok in warm water for 5–10 minutes. After soaking, the rust should remove itself, enabling typical wok cleaning. Steel wool can be used to scour your wok free of stubborn rust. However, seasoning your wok again after eliminating corrosion with steel wool or other abrasives will restore its patina.

## Best Oil for Wok

The finest oils for a wok can be used at high temperatures without burning because they have a high smoking point. They must impart a neutral flavor and be refined. Avoid unrefined oils with low smoking points, like sesame oil and olive oil. Instead, pick one of these oils to season your wok:

- Grape seed oil
- Peanut oil
- Lard or pork fat
- Canola oil
- Sunflower oil
- Shortening

The patina will emerge, and the efficacy of the pan will increase as you use the wok. Food will release from the pan effortlessly and rapidly as its non-stick qualities improve. Food particles will be less likely to stick, making cleaning easier. With proper care, your wok will last you for many years.

# CHAPTER 3

# POPULAR COOKING METHODS FOR ASIAN CUISINE

The most common cooking methods used in Asian cuisine are listed here, along with some famous dishes used.

## These are the top Asian cooking techniques.

### 1. Stir-frying

Stir-frying involves cooking your ingredients in a wok over high heat. A wok is a shallow bowl-shaped cooking pan with handles. Due to the unusual form, heat can be distributed evenly in the bottom, and the deeper sides make it simpler to stir or toss the ingredients.

A small amount of heated oil is needed for this method of cooking. Also, the cooking takes only a little while. Popular dishes prepared with this technique include fried rice, pad-thai, and beef broccoli stir-fries.

### 2. Deep frying

Deep frying is the process of cooking food in extremely hot oil. This results in a crispy, golden-brown exterior. Deep frying is frequently done with a wok because it causes less mess as its edges flare out to capture oil droplets. Also, it is easy to move around, exposing the meal to hot, fresh oil.

Deep-fried dishes include crackers, wontons, and Chinese spring rolls. Deep-fried dessert dishes include sesame balls and banana fritters.

### 3. Grilling

Grilling involves cooking food below or above a heat source. One typical example is over a charcoal fire. The food sears under direct heat, giving it a distinctive flavor and pleasing texture. The fat and the cut's size determine the quality of grilled meals.

Before grilling, food is sometimes wrapped in aluminum foil or leaves in some Asian countries. Yakitori from Japan, satay from Malaysia, and pan-grilled pork belly from the Philippines are a few Asian delicacies that utilize this technique.

## 4. Simmering

Simmering involves placing ingredients in moderate or low heat with liquid. This enables the food to absorb the seasoning while also gradually softening it. With little steam, tiny bubbles develop and rise to the top. Fish and other delicate proteins are best cooked with this technique.

Sinigang is an example. The tamarind flavor is cooked with meat, fish, and veggies. Another dish that mixes meat and vegetables in a flavorful curry sauce is Japanese curry.

## 5. Braising

This slow-cooking technique involves scorching the meal at a high temperature. It is prepared in a covered pot with a small amount of liquid. Tough slices of meat can be improved and softened with this cooking technique. Braised trotters, pig belly, and short ribs are among the most well-liked Chinese-inspired meals.

## 6. Steaming

Steaming heats and cook food utilizing the hot steam from boiling or simmering water. Unlike other cooking techniques, the food is not in contact with the water. It is put in a steamer basket above a pot of simmering or boiling water.

Steamed food is often moist and tender. In several Asian recipes, the food is wrapped in bamboo steamers or banana leaves. Dim sum, vegetables, and dumplings are some common Asian foods that use steam.

## 7. Roasting

When roasted, it is either hung over an open flame or cooked in an extremely hot oven. It is first washed and seasoned before basting with edible oil to keep the moisture in the meat during cooking. Vegetables and roasted meat are mostly juicy and crispy on the outside.

The texture and taste of the meal are enhanced by this cooking method. Roast chicken, Peking duck, and pork char siu are popular examples. Asian food is quite varied. While each country gives its cuisine a unique twist, they all use similar cooking techniques. So go ahead and whip up a meal in your kitchen and get the best of Pan-Asian cuisine with our **100 best recipes.**

# CHAPTER 4

# PAN ASIAN RECIPES

## JAPAN

### 1. ZOSUI (JAPANESE RICE SOUP)

Zosui is a hearty Japanese rice soup with pantry-ready ingredients like leftover ingredients, precooked rice, and eggs. The simple template is flexible while ensuring you have a satisfying meal at the end of the day.

| PREP TIME | COOK TIME | TOTAL TIME | SERVINGS |
|---|---|---|---|
| 10 Minutes | 20 Minutes | 30 Minutes | 2 |

## INGREDIENTS

**For Broth**
- 3 cups dashi (I use three cups water + one dashi packet; for vegetarian/vegan, make Vegan Dashi)
- ½ teaspoonful kosher salt (Diamond Crystal; use half for table salt)
- 2 teaspoonful usukuchi (light-colored) soy sauce

**For Zosui**
- 1 inch carrot (1.4 oz, 40 g)
- 6 oz boneless, skinless chicken thighs (you can use 1-2 pieces depending on the size)
- 2 shiitake mushrooms (2.8 oz, 80 g)
- ½ tsp toasted white sesame seeds
- 1½ cup Japanese short-grain rice (cooked) (10.6 oz; 1 rice cooker cup (180 ml, 150 g) yields 330 g of cooked rice, about two rice bowls; here we have about 1½ rice bowls.)
- 2 green onions/scallions
- ⅛ tsp white pepper powder
- One large egg (50 g w/o shell)

## INSTRUCTIONS

Gather all ingredients.
Getting the Dashi ready

1. Pour dashi broth into a big pot (I used a donabe). I explain how to prepare dashi using a dashi package in this recipe. Fill the donabe with water and a packet of dashi.
2. With the cover on, steadily heat the water to boiling point. After some minutes, open the cover and shake the bag to release extra flavor.
3. Cover the lid and keep heating the broth. Boil for 3 minutes, then remove and discard the dashi packet. Close the lid and set it aside.

## Getting the Ingredients Ready

1. Remove any extra fat from the chicken before cutting it into bite-sized pieces.
2. Slice the shiitake mushrooms caps very thinly, discarding the stiff stem.
3. Quarter the carrot lengthwise, then slice it thinly.
4. Slice the green onions very thinly and place them in a little bowl. We garnish with them at the end.
5. To remove extra starch from cold cooked rice, place it in a fine-mesh strainer, then rinse it under running water. Shake thoroughly and drain. Skip this step if you are using freshly made rice.

## To Prepare Zosui

1. Add the chicken to a hot dashi broth.
2. Cover the lid and heat it to a boil over low heat. After boiling, skim the foam and scum on the surface.
3. Add the carrot and cook it covered for 4-5 minutes or until soft.
4. Season the soup with salt and soy sauce when the carrot is fully cooked.
5. Include cooked rice that has been well-drained and shiitake mushrooms. Cook for 10 minutes with a cover on.
6. Beat the egg in a bowl.
7. Slowly sprinkle the beaten egg over the top to give the soup a frothy texture.
8. Add some green onion and sesame seeds. At the very end, add some white pepper powder.
9. Put the cover on the pot and move it to the table to be served in separate bowls.

| NUTRITION |
| --- |
| • Carbohydrates: 43 g  • Calories: 337 kcal  • Protein: 24 g  • Trans Fat: 1 g  • Fat: 6 g  • Cholesterol: 174 mg  • Potassium: 373 mg  • Fiber: 1 g  • Sodium: 728 mg  • Saturated Fat: 2 g  • Sugar: 1 g  • Vitamin A: 487 IU  • Calcium: 40 mg  • Vitamin C: 2 mg  • Iron: 4 mg |

## 2. YAKI UDON (JAPANESE STIR-FRIED UDON NOODLES)

Yaki Udon is a Japanese dish that consists of udon noodles stir-fried with your choice of protein, veggies, and sauces. It's simple to make this recipe vegan or vegetarian. It takes 25 minutes to prepare and is delicious!

| PREP TIME | COOK TIME | TOTAL TIME | SERVINGS |
| --- | --- | --- | --- |
| 10 Minutes | 15 Minutes | 25 Minutes | 2 |

## INGREDIENTS

- 2-3 leaves green cabbage (8 oz, 227 g)
- ½ onion (3.5 oz, 100 g)
- Two shiitake mushrooms (0.7 oz, 20 g)
- 2 inches carrot (1.8 oz, 50 g)
- Two green onions/scallions
- 6 oz sliced pork belly (use your choice of seafood or meat; omit for vegan/vegetarian and use mushrooms, tofu, or extra vegetables instead)
- 2 servings udon noodles (180g/6.3 oz dry udon noodles; 1.1 lb/500 g frozen or parboiled udon noodles)
- 1 Tablespoon neutral-flavored oil (rice bran, vegetable, canola, etc.) (for cooking)
- ⅛ teaspoon kosher salt (Diamond Crystal; use half for table salt)
- ⅛ teaspoon freshly ground black pepper

## For the Seasonings Option A

- 2 Tablespoon soy sauce
- ½ teaspoon dashi powder (use kombu dashi powder for vegan/ vegetarian or skip)
- 1 teaspoon mirin (or a pinch of sugar)
- 1 Tablespoon's sake

## For the Seasonings Option B

- 1 teaspoon soy sauce
- 3 Tbsp mentsuyu/tsuyu (concentrated noodle soup base)

## For the Garnish (Optional)

- 3 Tablespoon katsuobushi (dried bonito flakes) (or one to two little packages of katsuobushi; skip for vegan/ vegetarian)
- 2 Tablespoon pickled red ginger (kizami beni shoga or beni shoga)

## INSTRUCTIONS

Gather all the ingredients. I chose Seasonings Option A for this dish presentation. Start boil a big pot of water over medium-high heat to blanch or cook the udon noodles.

### Getting the Ingredients Ready

1. Thinly slice the onion.
2. The cabbage leaves' tough core should be removed. Then, trim the leaves into pieces about 1 inch (2.5 cm).
3. Peel the carrot and cut it carrot into thin slices. After that, julienne them into two inches (5 cm) long strips.
4. Slice the mushroom tops and discard the rough shiitake stems.
5. Green onions should be divided into 2-inch (5-cm) pieces. Slice the pork belly into 2.5 cm (1 inch) thick chunks.
6. The frozen udon should be blanched in boiling water for 30 to 40 seconds or until it barely begins to defrost. Use dried udon noodles and cook them per the package's directions. Put the noodles on a platter and set aside.

## To Stir-Fry

1. A big frying pan should be heated to medium. Spread the oil evenly after adding it to the heated pan. Add the pork and stir-fry.
2. Add salt and freshly ground black pepper to season the pork. Cook until it stops being pink.
3. Sliced onions should be added and stir-fried until tender.

4. Add the green onions, shiitake mushrooms, carrot strips, and cabbage. Combine all ingredients until they are coated with oil.

5. Reduce the heat to low and cover it with a lid. 3 minutes of steaming the ingredients are enough to wilt them gently.

6. Udon noodles should be added to the pan and mixed using a pair of tongs (it's much easier to use tongs than two spatulas).

7. Choose options A or B for the ingredients and add those ingredients to the pan. Try option B, my go-to seasoning if you have mentsuyu at home; it's easy and excellent.

8. Mix everything. Taste the seasoning, and add extra salt and more ground black pepper to your preference.

## To Serve

Place the Yaki Udon on separate plates. Optionally garnish with red pickled ginger on the side and add bonito flakes.

## To Store

The leftovers should be stored in an airtight container for three to four days in the fridge and a month in the freezer.

### NUTRITION

• Carbohydrates: 59 g • Protein: 26 g • Calories: 976 kcal • Fat: 67 g • Polyunsaturated Fat: 10 g • Saturated Fat: 23 g • Monounsaturated Fat: 30 g • Cholesterol: 82 mg • Trans Fat: 1 g • Sodium: 938 mg • Fiber: 6 g • Sugar: 6 g • Potassium: 445 mg • Vitamin A: 5228 IU • Calcium: 51 mg • Vitamin C: 7 mg • Iron: 2 mg

## 3. TOSHIKOSHI SOBA (NEW YEAR'S EVE SOBA NOODLE SOUP)

Eat a steaming bowl of Toshikoshi Soba to usher in the New Year per Japanese custom. This basic Japanese noodle dish will make the previous year's struggles disappear and embrace the journey ahead!

| PREP TIME | COOK TIME | TOTAL TIME | SERVINGS |
|---|---|---|---|
| 10 Minutes | 20 Minutes | 30 Minutes | 2 |

## INGREDIENTS

• 7 oz dried soba noodles (buckwheat noodles)

### For the Soba Broth (from scratch)

• One piece kombu (dried kelp) (10 g; 4 inches x 4 inches, 10 x 10 cm)
• Three cups water (for vegetarian/ vegan, you can skip katsuobushi or make Vegan Dashi)
• One Tablespoon's sake
• ¼ tsp kosher salt (Diamond Crystal; use half for table salt)

13

- 2 Tablespoon mirin
- One cup katsuobushi (dried bonito flakes) (skip for vegetarian/vegan)
- Two Tablespoon usukuchi (light-colored) soy sauce

## For the Toppings

- 4 slices kamaboko (fish cake) (skip for vegan/ vegetarian)
- 2 Tablespoons dried wakame seaweed
- shichimi togarashi (Japanese seven spice)
- One green onion/scallion

## For the Quick Soba Broth (with concentrated mentsuyu; optional)

- ⅓ cup mentsuyu/tsuyu (concentrated noodle soup base)
- 2⅓ cups water
- 1 Tablespoon mirin

## INSTRUCTIONS

Gather all ingredients. Soak the kombu in water over the night (optional). If there isn't enough time, get the kombu soaking as soon as possible. Bring a pot of water to a boil for the soba noodles.

## To Make Soup Broth

1. Mix Cold brew kombu dashi, known as kombu, and water in a medium saucepan. Bring everything to a boil gradually over low heat (so kombu dashi will have more flavor). Discard the kombu once the water has come close to a boil (you can make furikake rice seasoning with the leftover kombu).
2. Add katsuobushi, then simmer for thirty seconds. Once the heat has been turned off, let the katsuobushi settle to the bottom of the pan. Steep for around 10 minutes (meanwhile, you can prepare the toppings).
3. Discard the katsuobushi and drain the dashi into the measuring cup (or basin) (you can make furikake rice seasoning with the leftover katsuobushi). Refill the saucepan with the dashi.
4. Add the usukuchi soy sauce, sake, kosher salt, and mirin.
5. Bring it to a simmer. When the mixture boils, turn off the heat, cover, and set aside.

## To Prepare Toppings

1. Rehydrate wakame seaweed cup water. The water will then be squeezed out and stored aside.
2. Slice the green onion very thinly.
3. Remove the bottom of the kamaboko (fish cake) from the wooden board, then slice four thin pieces.

## To Cook Soba Noodles

1. Soba noodles should be prepared per the directions on the package in a pot of boiling water. Unlike pasta, the water doesn't need to be salted.
2. Drain the soba noodles and rinse them in cool water to remove the starch. Put the noodles in separate bowls.

## To Serve

1. Pour hot soup broth over the soba noodles and top with wakame seaweed, kamaboko, and green onions. If desired, add shichimi togarashi. Enjoy while it's hot.
2. Making the Quick Soba Broth (with concentrated mentsuyu; optional)
3. Make the broth according to the directions on your mentsuyu bottle.

4.   Water, mentsuyu (noodle soup base), and mirin should all be thoroughly mixed in a medium saucepan. Simmer the mixture gently over medium heat. After turning off the heat, cover it with a lid. The soba broth is ready to use.

## NUTRITION

- Carbohydrates: 85 g  • Calories: 388 kcal  • Protein: 17 g  • Saturated Fat: 1 g  • Sodium: 761 mg  • Fat: 1 g
- Cholesterol: 3 mg  • Potassium: 308 mg  • Sugar: 6 g  • Vitamin A: 212 IU  • Fiber: 1 g  • Vitamin C: 2 mg
- Iron: 3 mg  • Calcium: 55 mg

## 4. EASY JAPANESE FRIED RICE (YAKIMESHI)

You can prepare this traditional Japanese fried rice (Yakimeshi), ham, eggs, and green onions, in under 20 minutes. It's delicious to the brim and ideal for a weeknight meal.

| PREP TIME | COOK TIME | TOTAL TIME | SERVINGS |
| --- | --- | --- | --- |
| 5 Minutes | 10 Minutes | 15 Minutes | 2 |

## INGREDIENTS

- Two rice bowls cooked Japanese short-grain rice (1¾ cups, 12 oz; cooled; day-old rice, preferably; if you have not prepped the rice yet, cook one rice cooker cup of short-grain rice and follow the instructions below)
- One green onion/scallion
- Two slices ham
- 2 teaspoon soy sauce
- One large egg (50 g w/o shell)
- ½ teaspoon kosher salt (Diamond Crystal; use half for table salt)
- 2 Tablespoon neutral-flavored oil (rice bran, vegetable, canola, etc.) (divided)
- ⅛ teaspoon white pepper powder

## INSTRUCTIONS

### To Prepare the Ingredients

1.   The leftover cooked rice from the previous day can be reheated in the microwave until it is warm or at room temperature. Put the two servings of newly cooked rice on a baking sheet. Allow it to cool completely before picking it up. This will remove the moisture from the rice.
2.   Cut the green part of the green onion diagonally and the white part into rounds. Do not mix the white and green parts. Set a few of the green slices aside for the garnish.
3.   Cut the ham into 1/2-inch (1.3-cm) square.
4.   Crack the egg and whisk in a bowl.

## To Cook the Fried Rice

1. To avoid delays, have everything ready as this meal moves swiftly through the cooking process. Preheating the wok (or big frying pan) over medium heat. Add half of the oil and swirl to cover the bottom and sides when the wok is heated. Add the beaten egg to the heated wok. The egg will float on top of the oil after a few seconds.
2. Use the edge of a spatula to gently move the loosely set egg around the pan, which will help it cook more evenly while maintaining its fluffy texture. When the bottom of the egg is set, but the top is still slightly runny and fully cooked, move it to a plate. Try not to overcook the egg at this point.
3. Add the remaining oil to the pan. After that, mix in the ham and the whites of the green onions. Coat everything in oil and stir-fry.
4. Put the cooled, cooked rice into the wok. Use a slicing motion with the spatula to break apart the rice clumps without breaking the rice grains. Toss the rice so it becomes coated with oil and gets a lovely sear, then add it to the ham mixture and continue tossing.
5. Return the cooked egg to the wok, breaking it into smaller pieces as you do so, and mix it in with the rice. If any rice sticks to the wok (which occurs when there isn't enough oil), a well-seasoned or nonstick wok will make it easy to scrape it off. This creates a nice charred flavor. The rice may require extra oil using a stainless-steel pan because it sticks more easily.
6. Add salt and pepper to the rice.
7. Toss the rice with soy sauce so that it is well distributed. The idea is to toss the rice in the air constantly, so it cooks evenly and does not stay together at the bottom of the wok. The smoky flavor of the rice can be enhanced by turning and tossing it in the air.
8. Add the green part of the chopped green onion. Taste fried rice and adjust the seasoning as required. Give the rice a few more toss, then transfer it to a plate.

## To Serve

In Japanese Chinese restaurants, the fried rice is typically shaped like a dome. To serv, fill a rice bowl with the fried rice, softly pat it down to compact it, and then flip it onto a dish. Fill the rice bowl and use it for the other plate. When ready to serve, sprinkle the sliced green onion and set aside.

## To Store

Refrigerate leftovers for up to two days or freeze them for up to a month in an airtight container.

**NUTRITION**

• Carbohydrates: 28 g • Calories: 318 kcal • Saturated Fat: 4 g • Protein: 9 g • Fat: 19 g • Polyunsaturated Fat: 9 g • Trans Fat: 1 g • Cholesterol: 102 mg • Monounsaturated Fat: 5 g • Fiber: 1 g • Sodium: 719 mg • Sugar: 1 g • Potassium: 115 mg • Vitamin A: 195 IU • Vitamin C: 1 mg • Iron: 2 mg • Calcium: 21 mg

## 5. GYUDON (JAPANESE BEEF RICE BOWL)

Gyudon is a popular dish that consists of thinly sliced beef and soft onions cooked in a savory-sweet sauce. It became an indispensable part of Japanese cuisine more than 150 years ago.

| PREP TIME | COOK TIME | TOTAL TIME | SERVINGS |
|---|---|---|---|
| 5 Minutes | 15 Minutes | 20 Minutes | 2 |

## INGREDIENTS

- 1 green onion/scallion
- ½ onion (4 oz, 113 g)
- ½ lb thinly sliced beef (chuck or rib eye)

### For the Sauce

- ½ cup dashi (Make Vegan Dashi for vegan/vegetarian)
- 3 Tbsp soy sauce
- 1 Tablespoon sugar (adjust according to preference)
- 2 Tablespoon mirin (substitute with two Tablespoons water/sake + 2 teaspoon sugar)
- 2 Tablespoon's sake (substitute with dry sherry or Chinese rice wine; use water for a non-alcoholic version)

### For Serving

- 2 servings cooked Japanese short-grain rice (1½ rice cooker cups (180 ml x 1.5 = 270 ml) yields about 2 servings (3 US cups)
- pickled red ginger (kizami beni shoga or beni shoga) (to garnish)

## INSTRUCTIONS

1. Gather all the ingredients. I normally place the thinly sliced beef in the freezer for ten minutes for easy cutting.
2. To begin, slice the onion very thinly.
3. Next, thinly slice the green onions on the diagonal.
4. Next, get the meat from the freezer. The sliced meat should be cut into pieces 3-inch (7.6 cm) wide.
5. Don't turn on the heat yet, but put the dashi, mirin, soy sauce, sake, and sugar in a large frying pan. Mix well.
6. The onion slices should next be added and evenly distributed throughout the pan with some space between each layer.
7. After that, place the meat over the onions. Cut the beef into thin slices, then separate them so they can wrap around the onions.
8. Cover the pan and cook over medium heat.
9. After cooking the meat, strain the broth through a fine-mesh skimmer to remove any scum or fat. Reduce the heat and cook for another three to four minutes.
10. Cover for a further minute and sprinkle with green onions. At this point, you might choose to add beaten eggs.
11. Place the steamed rice in a large donburi bowl and top with the remaining sauce.

12. Add the beef and onion mixture. You can add the leftover sauce on top if you like. Top with the pickled red ginger.

## To Store

Any leftover egg mixture and beef can be stored in an airtight container for up to two days in the refrigerator or three to four weeks in the freezer.

| NUTRITION |
| --- |

• Calories: 453 kcal  • Protein: 27 g  • Carbohydrates: 41 g  • Fat: 16 g  • Polyunsaturated Fat: 1 g  • Saturated Fat: 7 g  • Monounsaturated Fat: 8 g  • Sodium: 1072 mg  • Potassium: 432 mg  • Cholesterol: 69 mg  • Fiber: 1 g  • Vitamin A: 23 IU  • Vitamin C: 4 mg  • Sugar: 10  • Iron: 4 mg g  • Calcium: 24 mg

## 6. OYAKODON (CHICKEN AND EGG RICE BOWL)

Oyakodon is a classic Japanese home-cooked dish for relaxation and comfort. Chicken, onion, and eggs are simmered in a dashi-based sauce that's rich in umami, and then the whole thing is poured over a bowl of fluffy steamed rice. This is a quick and easy 30-minute meal that's simple to prepare yet still tastes great and brings you comfort.

| PREP TIME | COOK TIME | TOTAL TIME | SERVINGS |
| --- | --- | --- | --- |
| 15 Minutes | 10 Minutes | 25 Minutes | 2 |

## INGREDIENTS

- 10 oz boneless, skinless chicken thighs (the weight of a thigh varies: You need one or two thighs for two servings; if a thigh weighs 142-170 g or 5-6 oz, use two pieces; use plant-based meat substitute for vegetarian/vegan)
- ½ onion (4 oz, 113 g; peeled)
- 3-4 large eggs (50 g each w/o shell) (for vegetarian/ vegan, use egg substitute such as JUST Egg)
- 1 Tablespoon's sake (for marinating the chicken; sake aids the removal of the chicken's gamey odor; you can also use dry sherry or Chinese rice wine, or otherwise, skip it)

## For the Seasonings

- ½ cup dashi (using good, flavorful dashi is essential; for vegetarian/ vegan, make Vegan Dashi)
- 2 Tablespoon mirin
- 2 Teaspoon sugar
- 2 Tablespoon soy sauce

## For Serving

- Two servings cooked Japanese short-grain rice (1½ rice cooker cups (180 ml x 1.5 = 270 ml)

18

- shichimi togarashi (Japanese seven spice) (optional)
- Four sprigs mitsuba (Japanese parsley) (or scallion/green onion)
- Japanese sansho pepper (optional)

## INSTRUCTIONS

### Before You Start

The use of both a standard-sized (about 10 inches/25 cm) frying pan and a smaller (about 8 inches/20 cm) oyakodon pan are detailed in this recipe. Oyakodon is often prepared on an oyakodon pan, allowing the cooked ingredients to be easily put onto the rice bowl when serving. For specific preparation steps, please refer to the recipes listed below.

Collect everything you'll need. If you only have a medium-sized frying pan, don't try to create more than two servings at a time.

### To Prepare the Seasonings

Combine the dashi, mirin, sugar, and soy sauce in a liquid measuring cup or bowl. Stir until the sugar is dissolved.

### To Prepare the Ingredients

1. The onion should be sliced lengthwise into about a quarter of an inch (6 mm) broad.
2. Mitsuba or green onions should be chopped into pieces, ½ inch (1.3 cm) wide.
3. The chicken will taste better if you use a knife to remove the excess fat and connective tissue.
4. Strip the chicken thighs into pieces between ¾ to 1 inch (2-2.5 cm) wide, cutting along the grain. The chicken strips should be sliced against the grain into pieces around ¾ inch to 1 inch (2-2.5 cm) square using a knife held at a back and diagonal angle (almost parallel to the cutting board). Using this "sogigiri" cutting method, the chicken pieces are all the same thickness and have a larger surface area for rapid cooking and enhanced flavor absorption.
5. Place the chicken in a dish or on a plate and sprinkle with the sake. Set aside for five minutes.
6. Crack the eggs into a bowl. Chopsticks can "cut" the egg whites into smaller pieces five or six times. The egg whites won't get all spilled into the pan at once. Don't beat the eggs or mix them.
7. Tip: Aim for a meal in which the whites of the eggs stand out clearly against the yellow parts.
8. You may have accidentally broken some egg yolks while "cutting" the egg whites. That's OK. You can gently poke the yolks to break them if they haven't already, but you shouldn't mix the egg whites and yolks. The eggs should look like a marble pattern.

### To Cook the Oyakodon in a Medium Frying Pan

1. Slice the onions in a medium frying pan (I like a well-seasoned 11-inch carbon steel pan) in a single layer while the heat is turned off. Then, mix in the seasoning mix. It should cover the onions. If it doesn't, your frying pan is too big, or the spice must be adjusted.
2. Put it over medium heat and let it simmer for a few minutes. Once simmering, add chicken on top of the onions.
3. Distribute the onion and chicken evenly. Once simmering again, turn the heat down to medium-low. Cover and let simmer for five minutes, or until onions are soft and the chicken is no longer pink. Halfway through, flip the chicken.
4. A helpful hint: reducing the sauce by evaporation will bring out its full taste.
5. The eggs will be added in two stages: Two-thirds of the eggs and the remaining one-third later. Get the temperature up to medium. Two-thirds of the eggs should be drizzled over the chicken and onions in a circular motion while the cooking liquid is simmering (little bubbles around the edges of the pan), with care taken to avoid the corners of the pan where the eggs are more likely to overcook. As with traditional Egg

Drop Soup, the eggs should only be drizzled if the cooking liquid is simmering. Moreover, as egg whites require more cooking time than egg yolks, you should add extra whites now. For the best appearance, the yolks should remain runny and tender.

6. Put the heat down if it's too high. If the egg drifts toward the pan's edges, gently gather it towards the center of the pan, where the heat is less intense. Cover the pan if the egg whites take too long to set.

7. Add the remaining eggs to the center and the borders of the pan when they are just beginning to set but are still runny. Once the egg is cooked to your preference, sprinkle the mitsuba (or green onion) on top and continue to cook on medium-low. In Japan, oyakodon is typically served with an almost-set but still-runny egg (raw eggs are safe to consume in Japan). To ensure that the oyakodon has a brilliant yellow top, try to distribute additional egg yolks throughout the remaining one-third of the egg. Add a beaten extra yolk at the end for a good presentation.

8. Steamed rice should be served in separate bowls. Place the cooked chicken and egg combination on top of the steaming rice, then add as much pan sauce as you like.

## To Cook the Oyakodon in a Small Frying Pan or an Oyakodon Pan

1. Cook the egg and chicken in 2 batches, one serving at a time. The ingredients must be split in half. Add half the chopped onions to the pan in a single layer with the stove off. Add only half of the seasoning mixture (should cover the onions).

2. Set the temperature to medium and simmer the mixture. Add half of the chicken to the onions after it has begun to cook.

3. Ensure that the chicken and onions are distributed evenly. Reduce the heat to medium-low when it begins to simmer. Cook for 4 minutes with the lid off or until the onions are soft and the chicken is no longer pink. Halfway through, flip the chicken.

4. Tip: Evaporation aids in sauce reduction and taste intensification.

5. The eggs will be added in two steps: first two-thirds of the eggs, then the final one-third. The heat should now be set at medium. Drizzle two-thirds of the eggs over the chicken and onions when the cooking liquid is simmering (has little bubbles around the edges), and stay away from the pan's rims where the eggs might easily be overcooked.

6. Tip: Ensure the cooking liquid is simmering before adding the eggs. Also, add egg whites now, as they cook more slowly than the yolks. The yolks should ideally remain soft and runny for the presentation.

7. While the eggs are still runny but set, add the remaining eggs to the middle and the borders of the pan. When the egg is cooked to your preference, sprinkle the mitsuba (or green onion) on top and continue to cook on medium-low. In Japan, oyakodon is typically served with an almost-set but still-runny egg (raw eggs are safe to consume in Japan). The egg yolk should be distributed evenly throughout the remaining one-third of the egg so that the oyakodon has a brilliant yellow top. Add a beaten extra yolk at the end for a nice appearance.

8. Steamed rice should be served in a separate dish. Add the necessary pan sauce before sliding the cooked chicken and egg combination onto the steaming rice. When using the remaining ingredients, repeat Steps 1 through 6.

9. Serve the oyakodon with optional side dishes of shichimi togarashi and sansho pepper.

## To Store

Store the leftover in the fridge for up to two or three days if kept in an airtight container. Don't add the eggs if you plan to store in the freezer. Add eggs after you reheat it in the pan.

### NUTRITION

• Carbohydrates: 41 g • Calories: 496 kcal • Protein: 41 g • Fat: 13 g • Polyunsaturated Fat: 3 g • Saturated Fat: 4 g • Monounsaturated Fat: 5 g • Cholesterol: 414 mg • Trans Fat: 0.1 g • Sodium: 1197 mg • Fiber: 1g • Sugar: 11 g • Potassium: 578 mg • Vitamin A: 442 IU • Vitamin C: 4 mg • Iron: 4 mg • Calcium: 70 mg

# 7. TERIYAKI TOFU

This pan-fried Teriyaki tofu is deliciously tasty and crisp to the taste. Enjoy this Japanese cuisine as an appetizer or the main course when served with rice and a few of your favorite sides. Anyone can try this dynamic recipe; there are easy ways to make it vegan or gluten-free.

| PREP TIME | COOK TIME | TOTAL TIME | SERVINGS |
|---|---|---|---|
| 10 Minutes | 15 Minutes | 25 Minutes | 2 |

## INGREDIENTS

### For the Tofu

- ⅓ cup potato starch or cornstarch
- 14 oz medium-firm tofu (momen dofu)
- 2 Tablespoon neutral-flavored oil (rice bran, vegetable, canola, etc.)

### For the Homemade Teriyaki Sauce

- 2 Tablespoon mirin
- 2 Tablespoon's sake
- 2 Tablespoon soy sauce (You can use GF soy sauce for gluten-free)

### For the Toppings (optional)

- Pickled red ginger (kizami beni shoga or beni shoga) (to garnish)
- One green onion/scallion
- 1-2 packs katsuobushi (dried bonito flakes) (skip for vegan/vegetarian)

## INSTRUCTIONS

### Gather all ingredients.

1. [Thirty Minutes Before Cooking] Wrap the tofu with a paper towel, then place it between 2 baking sheets or plates. After that, place something heavy on top to press and drain the tofu for 20 to 30 minutes. Remove the water. Alternatively, microwave the tofu for two to three minutes after wrapping it in a paper towel.
2. In a measuring cup or small basin, add 2 tablespoons sake, 2 tablespoons mirin, and 2 tablespoons soy sauce to prepare teriyaki sauce.
3. Tofu should be cut into squares. It should be about ½ inches.
4. Chop green onion. Heat 1-2 tablespoons of oil over medium-high heat in a wok.
5. Place potato or cornstarch in a tray or dish and add to the heated oil. Add the starch on the tofu.
6. Shake off extra starch, then place the tofu chunks in the pan. Cook the tofu until the bottom is golden brown and crispy. Flip and cook the other side.
7. Pour in the Teriyaki Sauce once both sides are nicely brown.

8. Shake the pan after flipping the tofu to distribute the sauce. Add katsuobushi (dried bonito flakes), then turn off the heat.
9. Serve the tofu on the platter and garnish with pickled red ginger and green onions. Serve right away.

## NUTRITION

• Carbohydrates: 18 g  • Calories: 294 kcal  • Saturated Fat: 5 g  • Protein: 21 g  • Fat: 14 g  • Polyunsaturated Fat: 5 g  • Sodium: 315 mg  • Monounsaturated Fat: 3 g  • Potassium: 168 mg  • Sugar: 3 g  • Fiber: 3 g  • Vitamin A: 60 IU  • Vitamin C: 2 mg  • Iron: 3 mg  • Calcium: 262 mg

# 8. TAMAGOYAKI (JAPANESE ROLLED OMELETTE)

Tamagoyaki (Japanese rolled omelet), a delicious Japanese breakfast or side dish for your bento lunches, is sweet yet savory.

| PREP TIME | COOK TIME | TOTAL TIME | SERVINGS |
|---|---|---|---|
| 5 Minutes | 5 Minutes | 10 Minutes | 2 |

## INGREDIENTS

- 2 Tablespoon neutral-flavored oil (rice bran, vegetable, canola)
- 1½ sheets nori (dried laver seaweed) (for an omelet with nori in it; optional)

## Seasonings

- 2 teaspoon sugar
- 3 Tablespoon dashi (use Kombu Dashi for vegetarians)
- 1 teaspoon soy sauce (use GF soy sauce for gluten-free)
- Two pinch kosher salt (Diamond Crystal; use half for table salt)
- Three large eggs (50 g each w/o shell)
- 1 teaspoon mirin

## Garnish

- soy sauce
- 3 oz daikon radish (1 inch, 2.5 cm; I prefer to use the green top part because it is sweeter than the white part)

## INSTRUCTIONS

## Gather all ingredients.

1. Whisk the eggs in a bowl. Avoid overmixing; it is preferable to "cut" the eggs with chopsticks in a zig-zag pattern.
2. Combine and thoroughly mix the seasonings in a separate bowl.
3. Add the seasoning mixture to the eggs, then whisk. To make it simpler to pour the mixture into the frying pan, transfer it to a measuring cup with a spout and handle.

## Tamagoyaki Pan Technique

1.  Heat the pan over medium heat, then dip a folded paper towel in oil, and add oil. To see if the pan is hot, add a little egg mixture. The pan is ready when you hear a sizzling sound.
2.  Add a thin layer of the egg mixture into the pan and immediately tilt it to coat the whole cooking surface with the egg mixture.
3.  Poke any air bubbles to let the air out. Once the bottom of the egg has set but is still soft on top, roll the egg into a log shape from one side to the other, starting from the far edge of the pan and rolling toward the pan handle.
4.  Move the rolled omelet to the far side of the pan from where you started rolling it, and use a paper towel to dab extra oil into the pan, being sure to get beneath the omelet as well.
5.  The egg mixture should now be added in a thin layer, covering the pan's bottom once again. Lift the omelet carefully to spread the mixture underneath.
6.  Once the new egg layer has set and is still soft, start rolling it from one side to the other.
7.  Place the rolled omelet on the side where you started it, then add extra oil to the pan with a paper towel and under the omelet.
8.  The egg mixture should now be added in a thin layer, covering the pan's bottom once again. Lift the omelet carefully so that the mixture can spread underneath.
9.  Once the new layer of egg has set, roll it from one side to the other.
10. Repeat the process. This completes the third round.
11. This is the 4th round. Pour more egg mixture, ensuring it coats the pan's bottom thinly and extends under the rolled omelet.
12. Keep rolling it into a log shape. Lift the frying pan to regulate the temperature instead of adjusting the stove's heat. Be careful because the egg can stick to the frying pan if the heat is too low.

## This is the 5th round.

## This is the 6th and final round.

13. You can make the omelet lightly brown.
14. After removing the omelet from the pan, place it on a bamboo sushi mat. Roll the omelet up in the bamboo mat while it's hot to help it take shape. Allow it to stand for five minutes.

## Round Frying Pan Technique

1.  Heat the pan over medium heat, then dip a folded paper towel in the oil, then add some oil to the pan while it is hot. To test whether the pan is hot, add a little egg mixture. When you hear a sizzling sound, pour a small layer of the egg mix into the pan, immediately turning the pan to coat the whole cooking surface.
2.  Poke any air bubbles to let the air out. Roll the egg into a log shape from side to side, starting from the far edge of the pan and rolling toward the pan handle after the bottom of the egg has set but is still soft on top. You can add a half sheet of nori and then roll (optional).
3.  Place the rolled omelet on the far side of the pan from where you started rolling it, then use a paper towel to wipe extra oil into the pan, covering the omelet as well. The egg mixture should now be added in a thin layer, covering the pan's bottom once again. Lift the omelet carefully so that the mixture spreads the mixture underneath.
4.  Once the new layer of egg has set it has set, start rolling from side to side. It's not compulsory to do this, but I added another layer of nori sheet before rolling.
5.  Place the rolled omelet on the far side of the pan from where you started rolling it, then use a paper towel to wipe extra oil into the pan, covering the omelet as well. The egg mixture is added thinly, covering the pan's bottom again. Lift the omelet carefully to spread the mix underneath.

6. Once the new egg layer has set the roll, start rolling from side to side. Before rolling, you can another sheet of nori here. Continue until all of the egg mix have been used.

7. After removing the omelet from the pan, place it on a bamboo sushi mat. Roll the omelet up in the bamboo mat while it's hot to help it take shape. Allow it to stand for five minutes.

## To Serve

1. Cut the omelet into pieces ½-inch (1 cm)
2. Grate and peel the daikon. Squeeze the water out gently. Pour the soy sauce over the shredded daikon when serving the Tamagoyaki.

## To Store

The tamagoyaki can be kept in the freezer for up to two weeks if placed in an airtight container. Defrost overnight in the microwave or refrigerator.

---

**NUTRITION**

- Protein: 10 g  • Calories: 199 kcal  • Carbohydrates: 7 g  • Fat: 14 g  • Trans Fat: 1 g  • Cholesterol: 279 mg
- Saturated Fat: 8 g  • Sodium: 347 mg  • Fiber: 1 g  • Sugar: 6 g  • Potassium: 207 mg  • Vitamin A: 503 IU
- Calcium: 55 mg  • Vitamin C: 10 mg  • Iron: 2 mg

## 9. JAPANESE EGG SANDWICH (TAMAGO SANDO)

The Japanese Egg Sandwich (Tamago Sando), which consists of egg salad sandwiched between two pieces of white bread, is a popular on-the-go snack available at every convenience store in Japan. The bread is soft and pillowy, while the filling is creamy and overflowing with the rich egg yolk flavor.

| PREP TIME | COOK TIME | RESTING TIME | TOTAL TIME | SERVINGS |
|---|---|---|---|---|
| 10 Minutes | 15 Minutes | 5 Minutes | 30 Minutes | 2 |

## INGREDIENTS

- 4 slices shokupan (Japanese milk bread)
- 3 large eggs (50 g each w/o shell)
- salted butter

## Seasonings

- ⅛ teaspoon freshly ground black pepper
- ¼ teaspoon sugar
- ¼ teaspoon kosher salt (Diamond Crystal; use half for table salt)
- 2 Tablespoon Japanese mayonnaise
- 2 teaspoon milk

## INSTRUCTIONS

Gather all ingredients.

## To Make the Egg Salad

1. Prepare the eggs by placing them in a medium saucepan, then add enough water to cover by one inch (2.5 cm). Get it boiling over medium heat. Cook for twelve minutes once boiling.
2. Stop the cooking process by moving the eggs into ice water as soon as they are done. Leave them to cool, and then peel the shells.
3. Put the peeled eggs in a dish and mash them with a fork. The egg whites should be mashed into uniformly sized bits.
4. Add the sugar and salt.
5. Add the milk and freshly ground black pepper. Season to taste with salt and pepper.
6. Add the mayonnaise and mix.

## To Assemble the Tamago Sando

1. Place two bread slices on the table. Spread the butter on both slices. Spread the egg salad evenly over one slice of bread.
2. Press the sandwich slightly by placing it between two plates with the top slice of bread buttered side down.
3. Set aside for five minutes.
4. Cut the crust off the bread.
5. Split the sandwich in half. Now, it's ready to serve.

## To Store

Any leftovers can be stored in the refrigerator for up to two days if sealed properly.

| NUTRITION |
| --- |

• Calories: 340 kcal  • Protein: 14 g  • Fat: 19 g  • Carbohydrates: 26 g  • Saturated Fat: 4 g  • Cholesterol: 285 mg  • Trans Fat: 1 g  • Sodium: 583 mg  • Fiber: 1 g  • Potassium: 170 mg  • Sugar: 4 g  • Calcium: 179 mg  • Vitamin A: 423 IU  • Iron: 3 mg

## 10. MISO BUTTER PASTA WITH TUNA AND CABBAGE

This Miso Butter Pasta with Tuna and Cabbage is a delightful fast dish with al dente pasta tossed with delectable Japanese seasoning. It simply requires common pantry ingredients and is ready in 15 minutes!

| PREP TIME | COOK TIME | TOTAL TIME | SERVINGS |
| --- | --- | --- | --- |
| 5 Minutes | 10 Minutes | 30 Minutes | 2 |

## INGREDIENTS

- 1 Tablespoon kosher salt (Diamond Crystal; use half for table salt) (for cooking pasta)
- 2 cloves garlic
- 7 oz spaghetti
- 5 oz green cabbage (3 leaves)
- 1 Tablespoon extra-virgin olive oil
- freshly ground black pepper
- 1 Tablespoon miso
- ½ (5-ounce) can albacore tuna (preferably packed in olive oil)
- 1 Tablespoon unsalted butter
- ¼ cup reserved pasta water
- 2 teaspoon mirin
- 2 teaspoon soy sauce

## INSTRUCTIONS

Gather all the ingredients.

### To Cook Spaghetti

1. In a big saucepan, boil 4 quarts (16 cups, 3.8 L) of water (I used a 4.5 QT Dutch oven). Add spaghetti and salt once the water starts boiling.
2. Spaghetti should be stirred to prevent sticking. Tip: I reduce the cooking time by one minute if I have to continue cooking the pasta later. If you cook the spaghetti first, you'll need to drain it, but you should be able to boil the remaining ingredients in 10 minutes as the spaghetti cooks.

### To Prepare Ingredients

1. While the pasta is cooking, we prepare the ingredients. Slice the peeled garlic cloves very thinly.
2. The cabbage's rough core should be removed before cutting into 1-inch square pieces.
3. Drain the tuna in the can. Using a big chunk, you can break/cut it into smaller pieces (optional).

### To Prepare Tuna and Cabbage, Japanese Pasta

1. Heat the olive oil in a big frying pan over medium heat. Add the garlic to begin infusing while the oil is still not hot. Make sure the garlic is well-oiled. Once the garlic is sizzling and thoroughly covered with oil, add the cabbage and coat with the oil for about two minutes.
2. Add the canned tuna, then toss it together with the cabbage.
3. Miso, unsalted butter, and freshly ground black pepper should be added. Allow the butter to melt while stirring to mix fully.
4. Reserve ¼ cup (60 ml) of pasta water and add to the frying pan.
5. Shake the pan to combine the ingredients. At this point in the mixing process, ensure the miso has dissolved.
6. Add the mirin and soy sauce.
7. Once the spaghetti has finished cooking, pick up the noodles with tongs (or drain them in the sink quickly), then add them to the pan. Toss the spaghetti to mix it all.
8. Add freshly ground pepper to the spaghetti. Taste and add salt if required. Serve the pasta in separate bowls. Enjoy!

## NUTRITION

• Calories: 569 kcal • Protein: 23 g • Fat: 15 g • Carbohydrates: 83 g • Saturated Fat: 5 g • Cholesterol: 29 mg • Trans Fat: 1 g • Sodium: 755 mg • Fiber: 5 g • Sugar: 7 g • Potassium: 444 mg • Vitamin A: 275 IU • Calcium: 72 mg • Vitamin C: 27 mg • Iron: 3 mg

## 11. NAPOLITAN (JAPANESE KETCHUP SPAGHETTI)

Need a family meal prepared in less than 20 minutes? Try this fast and simple Napolitan (Japanese Ketchup Spaghetti). This simple meal is made in homes and restaurants all over Japan, enhancing pantry staples with fresh ingredients like mushrooms, onions, sausages, and bell pepper. It's a delicious and satisfying dish!

| PREP TIME | COOK TIME | TOTAL TIME | SERVINGS |
|-----------|-----------|------------|----------|
| 5 Minutes | 15 Minutes | 20 Minutes | 2 |

## INGREDIENTS

- ¼-½ green bell pepper (2.5 oz or 70 g)
- ½ onion (100 g or 3.5 oz)
- Four mushrooms (70 g or 2.5 oz)
- 1 Tablespoon extra-virgin olive oil
- 5 oz sausages (I use 4-6 kurobuta or arabiki sausages from a Japanese grocery store; however, you can use any type of sausage, bacon, ham, etc.)
- 1 clove garlic
- ⅛ teaspoon freshly ground black pepper
- ¼ teaspoon kosher salt (Diamond Crystal; use half for table salt)

### For the Sauce

- 1 Tablespoon milk
- ⅓ cup ketchup (get a bottle of Kagome Tomato Ketchup from the Japanese grocery store for the authentic flavor)
- 2 teaspoon Worcestershire sauce
- ¼ cup reserved pasta water (you may not need it; please check your sauce and add gradually)
- 1 teaspoon sugar (for an authentic Japanese taste – option)

### For the Pasta

- 1½ Tbsp kosher salt (Diamond Crystal; use half for table salt)
- 7 oz spaghetti
- 1 Tablespoon unsalted butter

## For Serving

- 2 Tablespoon Parmigiano-Reggiano (Parmesan) cheese

## INSTRUCTIONS

Gather all ingredients. Get a big pot of water to boil.

## To Prepare the Ingredients

1. Combine and stir all the sauce ingredients in a small bowl.
2. Slice the onion into small pieces.
3. If the green bell pepper is long, cut it in half lengthwise, then into thin strips.
4. Cut the mushrooms thinly.
5. Slice the sausages thinly in a diagonal direction.

## To Boil the Spaghetti

1. Once the water has boiled, add the salt and spaghetti. Stir to prevent the noodles from sticking to each other. Follow the instructions on the spaghetti package for preparation. You'll set reserve some pasta cooking water toward the end of cooking.
2. While the pasta is cooking, make the sauce.

## To Cook the Sauce

1. Heat a big frying pan over medium heat. Once it's heated, add the oil and distribute it evenly. Use this garlic press to smash the garlic, then add it and sauté for one minute or until golden.
2. Add the onions to the pan and sauté for two to three minutes.
3. Once the onions have started to wilt, add the sausages and cook for one minute.
4. Add the mushrooms and bell peppers and sauté until everything is cooked.

## Add salt and pepper to taste.

1. Push the ingredients to one side, then add the sauce mix to the empty side of your pan. Once the sauce begins to bubble and thicken, mix it with the vegetables and sausages.
2. Scoop out roughly ¼ cup of the starchy cooking water from the pasta pot. Remember that you might not need the pasta cooking water you saved. You can only add it to the pasta sauce if it needs to loosen up. I occasionally use 1-2 Tbsp or don't use any at all. Once the sauce has reached the desired consistency, mix well while adding the reserved pasta water gradually.
3. Combine everything, then let the sauce boil and slightly thicken.
4. The spaghetti should be cooked by now. Drain it in a colander, then add it to the sauce-filled pan. Add the butter and mix using tongs, ensuring the sauce coats the pasta evenly.

## To Serve

The Napolitan should be served right away on separate plates. Sprinkle some Parmesan cheese over the pasta now or at the table.

## To Store

The leftovers can be stored in an airtight container and kept for 3 days in the refrigerator or 1 month in the freezer.

## NUTRITION

- Carbohydrates: 93 g  • Calories: 684 kcal  • Saturated Fat: 6 g  • Protein: 22 g  • Fat: 25 g  • Cholesterol: 23 mg  • Potassium: 776 mg  • Sodium: 673 mg  • Fiber: 6 g  • Vitamin A: 445 IU  • Vitamin C: 54 mg  • Sugar: 15 g  • Iron: 3 mg  • Calcium: 126 mg

## 12. VEGETARIAN RAMEN

Your world is about to be rocked by this vegetarian ramen! Learn how to make a creamy, rich broth with miso, sesame seeds, soy milk, and spicy chili bean sauce. You can simply convert this dish to vegan by skipping the egg!

| PREP TIME | COOK TIME | DASHI PREP (IN ADVANCE) | TOTAL TIME | SERVINGS |
|---|---|---|---|---|
| 10 Minutes | 20 Minutes | 30 Minutes | 1 Hr | 1 |

## INGREDIENTS

- ¾ cup water

### For the Vegetarian Dashi

- 1 piece kombu (dried kelp) (1 inch x 2 inches, 2.5 cm x 5 cm)

### For the Soup Broth

- 2 cloves garlic
- 1 Tablespoon toasted white sesame seeds
- ½ inch ginger
- 2 tsp roasted sesame oil
- green onion/scallion (white part)
- 2 teaspoons doubanjiang (broad bean paste. spicy chili bean sauce) (get a Taiwanese brand non-spicy doubanjiang for a non-spicy version)
- 1 Tablespoon's sake
- 2 teaspoon miso
- 2 teaspoon soy sauce
- ½ cup dashi
- One cup unsweetened soy milk
- Dash white pepper powder
- ¼ teaspoon kosher salt (Diamond Crystal; use half for table salt)

### For the Noodles

- 1 serving fresh ramen noodles (142-170 g or 5-6 oz fresh noodles; 90 g or 3.2 oz dry ramen noodles; use these GF ramen noodles for gluten-free)

## For the Ramen Toppings (Prepare Ahead)

- Spicy Bean Sprout Salad
- Ramen Egg (Ajitsuke Tamago) (omit for vegan)
- homemade vegetarian kimchi
- green onion/scallion (green part)
- frozen or canned corn

## INSTRUCTIONS

1. Gather all the ingredients. Please be aware that this recipe only yields one serving. You can scale the recipe to increase the ingredients if you want more servings.
2. To prepare the vegetarian Dashi (Kombu + Shiitake)
3. The calculated water should be used to soak the dried shiitake mushroom and kombu for at least thirty minutes. Add the liquid, shiitake, and kombu in a small saucepan. Over low heat, gradually bring the liquid to a boil. This will improve the flavor of the dashi.
4. Remove the shiitake mushroom and kombu from the dashi before it fully boils. The dashi will get slimy if you leave the kombu in the liquid. Switch off the heat and set aside.

## To Make the Soup Broth

1. Grind and smash the sesame seeds in a Japanese mortar and pestle.
2. Mince the ginger and the garlic (I used a garlic press).
3. Separate the white and green parts of the scallion, then into thin rounds.
4. Set a saucepan over medium-low heat. Once heated, add the sesame oil. Then, add the scallion's ginger, garlic, and white part. Cook until fragrant.
5. Miso and doubanjiang (spicy chili bean sauce/broad bean paste) should be added to the saucepan. Stir often to prevent burning.
6. With a wooden spatula, mix in the sake and scrape off any sauce globs stuck to the pan's bottom.
7. Add the soy sauce and ground sesame seeds.
8. Stir continuously as you add the soy milk to dissolve the doubanjiang and miso. Add the shiitake dashi and kombu.
9. Add a dash of salt and white pepper to taste. Switch off the heat and set aside.

## To Assemble

1. After preparing the soup and all the toppings, cook the fresh or dry ramen noodles in boiling water according to the directions on the package. (Don't cook the noodles for over 30–60 seconds.) Before putting the noodles in boiling water, loosen them and mix them to prevent sticking. At the same time, reheat the soup broth.
2. When the noodles have finished cooking, drain them thoroughly before adding them to a ramen bowl. Fill the bowl with the hot soup broth.
3. Place the preferred toppings on the ramen and enjoy!

## NUTRITION

- Carbohydrates: 63 g • Protein: 14 g • Calories: 549 kcal • Fat: 27 g • Sodium: 840 mg • Saturated Fat: 8 g • Potassium: 373 mg • Vitamin A: 219 IU • Vitamin C: 2 mg • Fiber: 4 g • Sugar: 2 g • Iron: 6 mg • Calcium: 238 mg

# 13. MISO RAMEN

You can prepare delicious Miso Ramen with real broth in less than 30 minutes! Please note that the toppings are optional. Preparation for Chashu and Ramen Eggs must begin a day ahead.

| PREP TIME | COOK TIME | TOTAL TIME | SERVINGS |
|---|---|---|---|
| 10 Minutes | 15 Minutes | 25 Minutes | 2 |

## INGREDIENTS

### For the Ramen Soup:

- 1 knob ginger (½ teaspoon grated ginger)
- 2 cloves garlic (1½ teaspoon minced garlic)
- 1 Tablespoon toasted white sesame seeds
- One shallot
- 1 Tablespoon roasted sesame oil
- 1 teaspoon doubanjiang (broad bean paste/ spicy chili bean sauce) (Get a Taiwanese brand non-spicy doubanjiang for a non-spicy version)
- 1 Tablespoon's sake
- 1 teaspoon kosher salt (use half for table salt) (adjust according to your chicken broth)
- ¼ lb ground pork
- Four cups Chicken Stock/Broth (store-bought or homemade) (each ramen bowl requires about 1½ cups (360 ml) of broth, plus a bit more for evaporation)
- 3 Tablespoon miso (each miso brand/type makes a slightly different broth)
- ¼ teaspoon white pepper powder
- 1 Tablespoon sugar

### For the Ramen and Optional Toppings:

- 2 servings fresh ramen noodles (283-340 g or 10-12 oz fresh noodles; 180 g or 6.3 oz dry ramen noodles; use these GF ramen noodles for gluten-free)
- Spicy Bean Sprout Salad (or blanched bean sprouts)
- Chashu (store-bought or homemade)
- Shiraga Negi (julienned long green onion)
- Ramen Egg (Ajitsuke Tamago)
- nori (dried laver seaweed) (cut a sheet into quarters)
- canned or frozen corn (drained)
- scallion/ green onion (chopped)

### For the Table (Optional):

- white pepper powder

- pickled red ginger (beni shoga or kizami beni shoga)
- la-yu (Japanese chili oil)

## INSTRUCTIONS

Gather all ingredients.

### To Prepare the Ramen Soup

1. Mince the ginger (I use this ceramic grater) and garlic (I use this garlic press).
2. Lettuce is minced. The three prepared components should be set aside.
3. The sesame seeds should be crushed, but some should remain whole for texture.
4. Heat the sesame oil over medium-low heat in a medium pot, and add the ginger, shallot, and minced garlic.
5. Stir-fry using a wooden spatula until fragrant.
6. Heat up to medium, then add the meat. Meat should be cooked until no longer pink.
7. Add the non-spicy bean paste (doubanjiang) or spicy bean paste (la doubanjiang) and miso. Quickly combine well with the meat before they burn.
8. Add sugar and ground sesame seeds, then mix thoroughly.
9. Add the chicken stock and sake, then bring the mix to a simmer.
10. After tasting your soup, season with salt and white pepper as needed. You should taste your soup to determine the appropriate amount of salt to use because the saltiness of each type of chicken stock differs.
11. While you cook the noodles, cover it with the lid and keep the ramen soup simmering

### To Prepare the Toppings and Ramen Noodles

1. Boil a large pot of unsalted water (ramen noodles already include salt in the dough). Once the water boils, pour little hot water into the serving bowls to warm them. In the meantime, lightly shake the fresh noodles to loosen and separate them.
2. Preparing the toppings in advance is crucial so you can serve the hot ramen immediately. For toppings, I use ramen egg, chashu, spicy bean sprouts (or blanched bean sprout), corn kernels, chopped green onion, shiraga negi, and a sheet of nori. Prepare some white pepper powder, a bottle of la-yu (chili oil), and a tiny dish of red pickled ginger on the table.
3. Noodles should be cooked as directed on the packaging. Normally, I prepare the noodles to be al dente (about fifteen seconds less than the suggested cooking time). Empty the hot water from the warmed ramen bowls before the noodles are cooked.
4. When the noodles are done, rapidly remove them with a mesh sieve from the water. Ensure you thoroughly drain the water because you don't want to dilute your soup. Noodles should be placed in the warmed bowls.
5. Add the ramen soup, then garnish with the prepared toppings.
6. Serve the noodles immediately after adding your preferred toppings.

**NUTRITION**

• Calories: 433 kcal • Protein: 19 g • Carbohydrates: 37 g • Trans Fat: 1 g • Fat: 25 g • Saturated Fat: 8 g • Cholesterol: 65 mg • Potassium: 341 mg • Fiber: 4 g • Sodium: 1216 mg • Sugar: 8 g • Vitamin C: 4 mg • Vitamin A: 112 IU • Iron: 4 mg • Calcium: 152 mg

## 14. BEEF UDON

Want a steamy bowl of hot noodle soup? I often turn to this comforting Beef Udon when I'm in dire need of Japanese food. In this recipe, chewy, thick udon noodles are topped with tender beef slices in a flavorful broth. What's not to love?

| PREP TIME | COOK TIME | TOTAL TIME | SERVINGS |
|-----------|-----------|------------|----------|
| 10 Minutes | 15 Minutes | 25 Minutes | 2 |

## INGREDIENTS

### For the Udon Broth from Scratch

- 2½ cups dashi (In this recipe, you'll learn how to make dashi utilizing a dashi packet and 2½ cups water. Make Vegan Dashi for vegans/vegetarians)
- 1 Tablespoon mirin
- 1½ Tablespoon soy sauce
- ⅛ teaspoon kosher salt (Diamond Crystal; use half for table salt)
- 1 teaspoon sugar

### For the Udon Noodle Soup

- 1 Tablespoon neutral-flavored oil (rice bran, canola, vegetable, etc.)
- 6-8 oz thinly sliced beef (rib eye or chuck)
- ½ Tokyo negi (naga negi; long green onion) (only the white part of the negi should be used; alternatively, use two green onions)
- 1 Tablespoon soy sauce
- 2 servings udon noodles (180 g or 6.3 oz dry udon noodles; 500 g/1.1 lb frozen or parboiled udon noodles)
- 2 teaspoon sugar

### For the Toppings

- One green onion/scallion
- Four stems mitsuba (Japanese parsley) (optional)
- shichimi togarashi (Japanese seven spice)
- Four slices narutomaki (fish cakes) (optional)

### For the Udon Broth (with Mentsuyu; Optional)

- 2⅓ cups water
- 1 Tablespoon mirin
- ⅓ cup mentsuyu/tsuyu (concentrated noodle soup base)

## INSTRUCTIONS

1. Gather all ingredients. For the udon noodles, heat a large pot of water to a boil. As soon as it begins to boil, maintain it at a low temperature until you are ready to cook the noodles.

## To Make the Udon Broth

1. Add the measured water and a dashi packet to a medium saucepan. It should boil when heated to a medium-low. If you have mentsuyu (a noodle soup base), prepare udon broth with mentsuyu by following the directions below.
2. Simmer for 2-3 minutes. Afterward, squeeze the dashi packet's liquid out and throw the package away.
3. Add the soy sauce, sugar, mirin, and salt, then mix it. Remove the soup from the heat and cover the pot with a lid to prevent it from evaporating.

## To Prepare the Ingredients

1. Slice the white part of the Tokyo negi into ½-inch (1.3 cm) diagonal pieces.
2. Thinly slice the tender stems and mitsuba leaves (optional).
3. Slice up the green onion thinly. Add the mitsuba and green onion slices to a small dish or bowl to top the soup later.
4. Narutomaki (fish cake) should be cut into four thin pieces diagonally. Cut the sliced shabu beef in half, about 1½ to 2 inches (3.8-5 cm) wide.

## To Cook the Beef

1. The frying pan should be heated to medium. Add the oil and negi once it's heated.
2. Once the negi is golden brown and soft, add the meat and heat it until it is no longer pink.
3. Add the soy sauce and sugar.
4. The meat should be stir-fried until well-seasoned. Remove from the heat.

## To Boil the Udon Noodles

1. Udon noodles should be prepared in boiling water per the directions on the package. For frozen udon noodles, boil from frozen for one minute to reheat. To get rid of extra starch, drain well and rinse quickly.

## To Serve

1. Divide the well-drained udon noodles into serving dishes, then top them with hot broth.
2. On top, scatter the stir-fried meat, narutomaki, green onions, and mitsuba. Sprinkle shichimi togarashi on top if you prefer it spicy. Enjoy!

## To Store

Stir-fried beef, udon noodles, and broth can all be kept separately in airtight containers and the fridge for up to three days.

## To Make the Udon Broth (with Mentsuyu)

Water, mentsuyu (noodle soup base), and mirin should all be thoroughly mixed in a medium saucepan. Over medium heat, simmer the mixture gently. After turning off the heat, cover it with a lid. The udon broth is ready to use.

**NUTRITION**

• Calories: 579 kcal  • Protein: 32 g  • Carbohydrates: 59 g  • Fat: 23 g  • Polyunsaturated Fat: 5 g  • Saturated Fat: 8 g  • Monounsaturated Fat: 9 g  • Cholesterol: 72 mg  • Trans Fat: 1 g  • Sodium: 976 mg  • Fiber: 4 g  • Sugar: 7 g  • Potassium: 353 mg  • Vitamin A: 107 IU  • Vitamin C: 2 mg  • Iron: 3 mg  • Calcium: 35 mg

# 15. MISO SALMON

This miso salmon recipe marinated in a sweet and savory miso sauce makes a fantastic weeknight meal. Enjoy Japanese ginger rice!

| PREP TIME | COOK TIME | MARINATING TIME | TOTAL TIME | SERVINGS |
|---|---|---|---|---|
| 5 Minutes | 10 Minutes | 1 Hour | 1 Hour 15 minutes | 2 |

## INGREDIENTS

- Two skin-on salmon fillets (1 lb, 454 g; cut in half if it is one big piece)

## For the Marinade

- 1 Tablespoon's sake
- ¼ tsp roasted sesame oil
- 1 Tablespoon mirin
- 2 Tablespoon miso (I use Hikari Miso Organic White Miso for this recipe: you can use any type of miso)
- 1 Tablespoon soy sauce

## For the Garnish (Optional)

- 1 green scallion/ onion (chopped)
- ½ teaspoon toasted white and black sesame seeds

## INSTRUCTIONS

Gather all ingredients.

1. Make sure your salmon fillets are free of tiny bones and scales. Check the skin with your fingers moving back and forth to see whether any scales are still there. Use a knife's flat side to scrape against the scales to get rid of them. Run your fingers down the flesh's surface and the sides to feel for any bones. You'll feel the hard tips of the bones poke your skin. To remove them, use fish bone tweezers. I advise cutting it in half to make the salmon fillet marinade and cook it more quickly.
2. Mix all ingredients for the marinade in a flat tray or large bowl.
3. Put the salmon in the bowl, skin side up. Coat the salmon skin with the marinade by spooning it on top. Cover it and put it in the refrigerator for one to two hours (a thicker cut need more time). Since miso is extremely salty, I do not advise marinating the salmon overnight for this lightly seasoned miso fish.
4. The oven should be preheated to 425°F (218°C) with the center rack in the oven. Reduce the cooking temperature by 25ºF (15ºC) for a convection oven. Remove the excess marinade entirely from the salmon, as miso burns easily.
5. Put the salmon slices on a baking sheet covered with parchment paper, skin side down. Put it into the thickest region of the salmon's flesh using an oven probe.

## To Bake the Salmon

1. Place the baking sheet into the oven, then attach the probe there. There is no need to turn the salmon during baking; bake it for about 18 to 20 minutes or until the thickest part of the fillet reaches an internal temperature of 125-130°F* (52-54ºC). I strongly advise purchasing a Thermapen instant-read thermometer if you don't already have one. Our suggested baking time without a thermometer is 5 min per ½-inch (1.3 cm) thickness of salmon (measured at the thickest). *At 120°F (49°C), you can stop cooking if you like medium rare. The USDA advises cooking fish to an internal temperature of 145°F (63ºC); nevertheless, the salmon will continue to cook from the residual heat, making the fish significantly overcooked.

2. This step is optional. We will broil the salmon to give it a lovely char. Take the probe out of the oven and the salmon. The oven should now be set to broil high (550°F/288°C), but the rack should remain in the middle and be 9 inches (23 cm) away from the top heating element. The salmon should be broiled on high for three minutes or until the surface is slightly browned and blistered. * You adjust the distance between the heating element and the food's surface while broiling rather than the oven's temperature. It is similar to using cooler and hotter zones on your grill.

3. I usually discard the marinade (thus why I use the least condiments); however, if you do not want to waste it or make too much, you can dilute it with water, then cook it for a few minutes. Use it in other meals or serve it with the salmon.

## To Serve

I served the ginger rice along with the salmon. Top the salmon with thinly sliced scallions and sesame seeds. Enjoy!

## To Store

The leftovers can be kept in an airtight container for up to three days in the refrigerator and a month in the freezer.

| NUTRITION |
|---|

• Calories: 308 kcal  • Protein: 40 g  • Carbohydrates: 3 g  • Fat: 13 g  • Polyunsaturated Fat: 5 g  • Saturated Fat: 2 g  • Monounsaturated Fat: 4 g  • Sodium: 423 mg  • Potassium: 1003 mg  • Cholesterol: 109 mg  • Vitamin A: 144 IU  • Vitamin C: 1 mg  • Fiber: 1 g  • Sugar: 1 g  • Calcium: 36 mg  • Iron: 2 mg

## 16. TERIYAKI SALMON

Prepare a tasty and light meal with the help of this quick and simple Teriyaki Salmon recipe any night of the week. Salmon fillets are pan-grilled to perfection using the old-fashioned technique, then topped with an homemade teriyaki sauce.

| PREP TIME | COOK TIME | TOTAL TIME | SERVINGS |
|---|---|---|---|
| 5 Minutes | 10 Minutes | 15 Minutes | 2 |

# INGREDIENTS

- ¼ teaspoon kosher salt (Diamond Crystal; use half for table salt)
- Two skin-on salmon fillets (340 g, 12 oz; ¾ inch (2 cm) thick; the skin will hold the flesh together while cooking)
- ⅛ teaspoon freshly ground black pepper
- ½ Tablespoon neutral-flavored oil (rice bran, vegetable, canola, etc.)
- 1 Tablespoon all-purpose flour (plain flour) (coating the salmon with flour helps it absorb the sauce and retain its juiciness and umami flavor; it also thickens the sauce; use potato starch or cornstarch for gluten-free)
- 1-2 Tablespoon's sake (for steaming; can substitute dry sherry, Chinese rice wine, or water; you may need the full amount for thick salmon fillets)
- 1 Tablespoon unsalted butter (for cooking)

## For the Teriyaki Sauce

- 1 Tablespoon's sake (can substitute dry sherry, Chinese rice wine, or water)
- 1 Tablespoon mirin (can substitute 1 Tablespoon sake/water + 1 teaspoon sugar for 1 Tablespoon mirin)
- 2 Tablespoon soy sauce
- 1 Tablespoon sugar

# INSTRUCTIONS

Gather all ingredients.

## To Make the Teriyaki Sauce

1. Mix all ingredients for the teriyaki sauce in a (microwave-safe) bowl and mix thoroughly.
2. Microwave the mixture for thirty seconds until the sugar is mostly dissolved.

## To Prepare the Salmon

1. The salmon fillets should be rinsed and dried. Use half the salt and half the pepper to season one side.
2. The second side should then be seasoned with the remaining pepper and salt.
3. Equally, distribute half of the all-purpose flour on one side of the salmon.
4. Turn it over and sprinkle the remaining flour on the reverse side. Give it a gentle press to adhere it, then remove any extra flour after.

## To Cook the Salmon

1. Heat the wok or a frying pan over medium heat. Add the oil and butter once the wok is heated. Make sure the butter doesn't burn. Reduce the heat or take the wok off the heat for a while if it becomes too hot. Sear the salmon fillets' skin one at a time. The skin should be pressed on the hot wok for fifteen seconds before the fillet is placed skin side down (also known as the "presentation side"). Because the first side to contact a clean pan will brown the most, the presentation side should go into the pan first. Repeat with the remaining salmon.
2. Turn the salmon over after 3 minutes or when the bottom is golden brown.
3. Add 1 tablespoon of sake (no more than 2 tablespoons for thicker fillets). Put a cover on the wok and lower the stove heat. Depending on the thickness of the fillets, steam the salmon for three to five minutes. If the sake has evaporated, but the salmon hasn't finished cooking, add another tablespoon of sake and keep steaming.
4. Cook the salmon until the thickest section of the fillet reaches an internal temperature of 125-130°F (52-54ºC) (I use a Thermapen instant-read thermometer). After that, move the salmon to a dish or tray. These fillets

were about ¾ to 1 inch (2-2.5 cm) thick and took about four minutes to cook. The USDA advises cooking fish to an internal temperature of 145°F (63°C); however, salmon must be removed from the heat t 125-130°F (52-54°C) to prevent overcooking.

5. Increase the heat and add the teriyaki sauce ingredients to the wok. Add the salmon back to the wok once the sauce starts to boil.

6. Spoon the sauce over the salmon. Once the sauce has thickened, turn off the heat. Move the salmon to a plate, drizzle the sauce on top, then serve immediately.

## To Store

The leftovers can be kept in an airtight container for up to 3 days in the refrigerator and for two weeks in the freezer.

| NUTRITION |
|---|

• Carbohydrates: 9 g • Calories: 274 kcal • Protein: 24 g • Polyunsaturated Fat: 3 g • Fat: 13 g • Saturated Fat: 5 g • Monounsaturated Fat: 4 g • Cholesterol: 77 mg • Trans Fat: 1 g • Sodium: 723 mg • Sugar: 6 g • Potassium: 565 mg • Fiber: 1 g • Vitamin A: 221 IU • Iron: 1 mg • Calcium: 17 mg

## 17. VEGGIE YAKI UDON

Pack in the veggies with our flavorful, Japanese-inspired yaki udon. It is nutritious, quick to prepare, and low in calories and fat.

| PREP TIME | COOK TIME | TOTAL TIME | SERVINGS |
|---|---|---|---|
| 10 Minutes | 15 Minutes | 25 Minutes | 2 |

## INGREDIENTS

- 1 red onion, cut into thin wedges
- 1½ tablespoon sesame oil
- 160g mangetout
- Three spring onions, sliced
- 70g baby corn, halved
- One large garlic clove, crushed
- Two baby pak choi, quartered
- 1 tablespoon pickled sushi ginger, chopped, plus 2 tablespoons of the brine, optional
- ½ tablespoon mild curry powder, or use 1 teaspoon garam masala
- 300g ready-to-cook udon noodles
- 4 teaspoons low-salt soy sauce

## INSTRUCTIONS

1. Heat the oil over high heat in a wok. Add the onion and fry for five minutes. Stir in the mangetout, pak choi, corn, and spring onions, then cook for five more minutes. Add the curry powder, soy sauce, and garlic, and cook for another minute.
2. Add the udon noodles, ginger (if using), and reserved brine. Stir in 2-3 tablespoons hot water until the noodles are heated. Divide in separate bowls and serve.

**NUTRITION: Per serving**

• Kcal: 366  • Protein: 15g  • Saturates: 1g  • Fat: 9g  • Carbs: 51g  • Fibre: 11g  • Sugars: 12g  • Salt: 1.4g

## 18. CHICKEN TERIYAKI

The famous Chicken Teriyaki, glazed in a savory homemade sauce, is incredibly juicy and tender when made according to the traditional Japanese method. No need for bottled teriyaki sauce!

| PREP TIME | COOK TIME | MARINATING TIME | TOTAL TIME | SERVINGS |
|---|---|---|---|---|
| 10 Minutes | 15 Minutes | 30 Minutes | 55 Minutes | 2 |

## INGREDIENTS

- ¼ onion (1 oz, 30 g)
- 1 knob ginger (1 inch, 2.5 cm)
- 1 teaspoon neutral-flavored oil (rice bran, vegetable, canola, etc.) (for step four of cooking the chicken)
- 1 lb boneless, skin-on chicken thighs
- freshly ground black pepper
- 2 Tablespoon's sake (for steaming)
- kosher salt
- 1 Tablespoon neutral-flavored oil (rice bran, canola, vegetable, etc.) (for step one of cooking the chicken)

### For the Teriyaki Sauce

- 1 Tbsp mirin
- 1 Tbsp's sake
- 1 Tbsp sugar
- 2 Tbsp water
- 2 Tbsp soy sauce

## INSTRUCTIONS

Gather all ingredients.

## To Make the Teriyaki Sauce

1. Combine the grated ginger, onion, and any juices in a large bowl.
2. Add all ingredients for teriyaki sauce in the bowl, then mix.

## To Prepare the Chicken

1. To help the chicken absorb flavor, prick it with a fork on both sides. If one side is thick, use a tenderizer or meat mallet to flatten the thighs.
2. Cut off extra skin and fat, then season chicken pieces with salt and pepper.
3. You can marinate the chicken for thirty minutes if you want to. Because the sauce might quickly burn, we don't often marinate the chicken in Japan before pan-frying it. Normally, I skip the marinating step and start cooking the chicken, and the teriyaki chicken is still delicious. I'll explain how to marinate and cook the chicken to emphasize certain essential guidelines while utilizing this optional technique.

## To Cook the Teriyaki Chicken

1. Heat a big frying pan over medium heat. Add the oil you measured for step 1 once the pan is heated. Remove as much of the marinade as you can to ensure that the chicken gets a great sear and does not end up steaming in the sauce. With the teriyaki marinade RESERVED, arrange the chicken skin-side down. If you can access a splatter screen, use it to reduce oil splatters, especially while cooking bacon and other oily foods.
2. Cook the chicken for three minutes. Flip the chicken over once the fat renders from the skin and the skin has turned golden brown. Add the sake, then immediately cover with a lid. Steam the chicken over medium-low heat for eight minutes.
3. Open the lid, then transfer the chicken to a plate. Wipe the pan clean of any extra grease.
4. Add the measured oil for step 4 and re-heat the pan over medium heat. Reposition the chicken in the pan with the skin side down. Brown and crisp the skin for an extra minute.
5. Turn the chicken so the skin side is facing up. Pour the teriyaki marinade that was reserved into the pan. Cook the sauce, regularly spooning it over the chicken, until it has roughly reduced by half. You can watch the sugar crystallize, and the sauce thickens as the alcohol from the mirin and sake evaporates. Turn off the heat.
6. Move the chicken to a cutting board, then bite it into pieces.
7. Serve with the leftover pan sauce drizzled on top and place on a plate.

## To Store

The leftovers can be kept for three days in the refrigerator or a month in the freezer in an airtight container.

**NUTRITION**

• Carbohydrates: 10 g  • Calories: 652 kcal  • Saturated Fat: 18 g  • Protein: 38 g  • Fat: 47 g  • Monounsaturated Fat: 17 g  • Trans Fat: 1 g  • Polyunsaturated Fat: 8 g  • Cholesterol: 222 mg  • Fiber: 1 g  • Sugar: 6 g  • Sodium: 849 mg  • Potassium: 521 mg  • Vitamin A: 177 IU  • Vitamin C: 1 mg  • Iron: 2 mg  • Calcium: 25 mg

## 19. AGEDASHI TOFU

Agedashi Tofu is a well-liked appetizer available in izakaya and Japanese restaurants. It is a crispy deep-fried tofu served with a savory umami sauce. While deep frying is required, the procedure is easier than you think. If you want to make it vegan, skip the bonito flakes!

| PREP TIME | COOK TIME | TOTAL TIME | SERVINGS |
|---|---|---|---|
| 15 Minutes | 15 Minutes | 30 Minutes | 2 |

## INGREDIENTS

- 4 Tablespoon cornstarch or potato starch
- 1 block medium-firm tofu (momen dofu) (397 g, 14 oz; use medium-firm tofu instead of the soft silken variety if this is your first time making this dish. It is easier to cook without breaking; if you prefer a silky texture, try silken tofu once you are more comfortable making Agedashi Tofu)
- Two cups neutral-flavored oil (rice bran, vegetable, canola, etc.) (You will need minimum 1 inch (2.5 cm) of oil in the pot)

### For the Sauce

- 2 Tbsp soy sauce
- One cup dashi (for vegetarian/vegan, make Vegan Dashi)
- 2 Tablespoon mirin

### For the Toppings

- 2 inches daikon radish
- Two green onions/scallions
- One knob ginger
- shichimi togarashi (Japanese seven spice) (optional)
- 1 package katsuobushi (dried bonito flakes) (skip for vegetarian)

## INSTRUCTIONS

Gather all ingredients.

1. Put the block of tofu on a dish or tray. Wrap the tofu in two to three layers of paper towels and place another tray on top. Put something heavy on top to press the tofu. The tofu should be completely dry after fifteen minutes.

### To Prepare the Toppings

1. Slice the green onions very thinly. Set aside.
2. Peel and grate the daikon.
3. Press the grated daikon to remove most of the water while retaining some moisture. Set aside.
4. Peel and grate the ginger. Set aside.

## To Make the Sauce

1. Add the soy sauce, dashi, and mirin to a small saucepan.
2. Simmer for a while. Once the heat is turned off, cover it with a lid and set it aside.

## To Deep-Fry

1. Heat the oil in a wok or medium saucepan to 320–340 °F (160–170 °C). Remove the paper towels from the tofu.
2. Cut the tofu block into six pieces.
3. Coat the tofu pieces with potato starch, dusting off excess.
4. Add the tofu chunks in batches once the oil is heated. I add three pieces at a time. Be careful not to overcrowd the pan. Deep-fry them until they are crispy and light brown, flipping them once.
5. To drain the excess oil, remove the fried tofu from the oil and set it on a wire rack or a dish lined with paper towels. Deep fry the remaining tofu pieces. After that, put the fried tofu in each serving bowl.

## To Serve

Pour the sauce slowly into each bowl, careful not to moisten the fried tofu's top. Add the grated daikon, ginger, and green onions as a garnish. If desired, top with katsuobushi and shichimi togarashi.

## To Store

The remaining sauce and fried tofu can be stored separately for three days in the refrigerator in airtight containers.

### NUTRITION

• Calories: 326 kcal  • Protein: 19 g  • Carbohydrates: 17 g  • Fat: 19 g  • Polyunsaturated Fat: 11 g  • Saturated Fat: 3 g  • Monounsaturated Fat: 5 g  • Sodium: 500 mg  • Trans Fat: 0.1 g  • Potassium: 155 mg  • Vitamin A: 10 IU  • Vitamin C: 4 mg  • Fiber: 3 g  • Sugar: 4 g  • Calcium: 261 mg  • Iron: 3 mg

## 20. CURRY UDON

This Curry Udon will quickly satiate your hunger for noodles thanks to its thick, chewy udon noodles and rich, fragrant curry soup. Bonus: You can quickly put it together on a busy weeknight.

| PREP TIME | COOK TIME | TOTAL TIME | SERVINGS |
|---|---|---|---|
| 10 Minutes | 40 Minutes | 50 Minutes | 2 |

## INGREDIENTS

- • 1 Tablespoon neutral-flavored oil (rice bran, vegetable, canola, etc.)
- • ½ onion (162 g or 5.7 oz)
- • 6 oz thinly sliced pork loin (you can use protein of your choice; cut into small pieces)

- 3 cups dashi (for vegetarian/ vegan, make Vegan Dashi)
- 1 Tablespoon's sake
- Two cubes Japanese curry roux (roughly 2 oz or 50 g; store-bought or made homemade Japanese curry roux)
- 2 servings udon noodles (180 g or 6.3 oz dry udon noodles; 1.1 lb or 500 g frozen or parboiled udon noodles)
- 2 teaspoon soy sauce

## For the Garnish

- 2 green scallions/ onions

## INSTRUCTIONS

1. Gather all ingredients. Use 2 pieces of the cubed curry roux; the rest can be kept in the refrigerator or freezer for one to three months if sealed in an airtight container. Prepare the dashi using your favorite method.
2. Slice the onion and green onions very thinly. Green onions should be set aside for garnish.
3. A medium-sized pot or Dutch oven (I used a 2.75 QT Staub) should be preheated to medium heat. Add the oil once the saucepan is heated. Next, add the onion slices.
4. Sauté the onion pieces for a couple of minutes. Add the meat next.
5. Cook the meat until it's barely pink. Add the sake next.
6. Add the dashi to the pot, then cover it with the lid. Cook for five minutes at a medium-low temperature.
7. Using a fine-mesh skimmer, remove the fat and scum from the stock while it is boiling and keep cooking.
8. Meanwhile, start boiling a large pot of water for the udon.
9. Once the stock and meat have simmered for five minutes, turn the heat off. In a ladleful of heated stock, add a cube of curry roux.
10. The roux cube should be thoroughly dissolved in the ladle using chopsticks or a spoon before being released into the soup. Take the next cube and repeat. Take your time to dissolve the curry roux fully because you don't want to consume any chunks of undissolved roux.
11. Add the soy sauce and mix. Turn off the heat and cover it with the lid to keep it warm.
12. Once the water is boiling, cook the udon noodles as directed on the package.

Drain the noodles and divide it into two bowls. Pour the curry soup on the udon noodles. Add the green onions on top, then serve right away.

**NUTRITION**

• Carbohydrates: 60 g  • Calories: 522 kcal  • Protein: 28 g  • Trans Fat: 1 g  • Fat: 12 g  • Saturated Fat: 10 g • Cholesterol: 56 mg  • Potassium: 451 mg  • Sodium: 1046 mg  • Fiber: 5 g  • Vitamin C: 5 mg  • Vitamin A: 120 IU  • Sugar: 5 g  • Iron: 2 mg  • Calcium: 44 mg

Yang Hong

## CHINA

## 1. SINGAPORE NOODLES WITH PRAWNS

This 20-minute low-fat, low-calorie variation of your preferred stir-fried takeaway is crammed with prawns and has a lot of flavors.

| PREP TIME | COOK TIME | TOTAL TIME | SERVINGS |
|-----------|-----------|------------|----------|
| 10 Minutes | 10 Minutes | 20 Minutes | 2 |

## INGREDIENTS

- 1 tablespoon light soy sauce
- 1 medium onion, sliced
- 1 tablespoon oyster sauce
- 1 yellow pepper or red pepper, cut into thin batons
- 2 nests thin vermicelli rice noodles
- 1 garlic clove, chopped
- 2 teaspoons mild curry powder
- 1 tablespoon sesame oil
- 1 red chili, thinly sliced (deseeded if you don't like it too hot)
- Eight raw king prawns
- thumb-sized piece of ginger, grated
- One large egg, beaten
- Four spring onions, cut in half lengthways, then into batons
- coriander leaves to serve

## INSTRUCTIONS

1. Rice noodles should be softened but not cooked after 5 minutes of soaking in warm water. Drain and set aside.
2. Mix the soy and oyster sauce in a small dish.
3. In a large wok, apply half the oil, then fry the garlic, ginger, and chili until golden, about two minutes. Stir-fry for a few minutes with the leftover oil, onion, spring onions, pepper, prawns, curry powder, and noodles. Put everything on one side, then mix the egg in. Add the soy sauce combination, stir for a few minutes, and then turn off the heat. Sprinkle the coriander leaves before serving.

## NUTRITION: per serving

• Fat: 10g   • Saturates: 2g   • Kcal: 411   • Carbs: 54g   • Fiber: 6g ·Protein: 23g   • Sugars: 10g   • Salt 2.6g

## 2. HEALTHY CHICKEN STIR-FRY

Prepare this nutrient-dense veg-packed stir-fry when you need a quick dinner. Add some chili to the rich peanut dressing if you like spice.

| PREP TIME | COOK TIME | TOTAL TIME | SERVINGS |
|-----------|-----------|------------|----------|
| 10 Minutes | 20 Minutes | 30 Minutes | 2 |

## INGREDIENTS

- 2 teaspoon rapeseed oil
- 65g brown basmati rice
- 15g ginger, peeled, then cut into thin matchsticks
- 160g broccoli, broken into florets, stem finely chopped
- Two small red onions (160g), cut into wedges
- 1 tablespoon crunchy peanut butter
- Two carrots (160g), halved lengthways and cut into diagonal slices
- 200g chicken breast, cut into thin strips
- One red chili, finely chopped (optional)
- ½ teaspoon ground cumin
- 1 tablespoon brown rice vinegar
- 1 tablespoon wheat-free tamari

## INSTRUCTIONS

1. Following the directions on the package, cook the rice, then drain. The ginger and red onions should be fried for two minutes in hot oil in a non-stick wok. If using, add the broccoli stem, carrots, and chili, then cook for a minute.
2. Stir-fry the chicken, cumin, and broccoli stems for a few seconds before adding 3 tablespoons of water. Cover and steam for 3–4 minutes until the chicken is cooked and the broccoli florets are tender.
3. Meanwhile, mix the peanut butter, vinegar, and tamari. Stir the sauce into the chicken and veg, then serve over the cooked rice.

**NUTRITION: Per serving**

• Fat: 13g  • Kcal: 465  • Protein: 35g  • Saturates: 1g  • Sugars: 15g  • Carbs: 47g  • Fibre: 10g  • Salt 1.3g

## 3. CRISPY CHILI BEEF

Instead of ordering takeout, prepare this Chinese-inspired flash-fried steak with red peppers and a sweet, gingery sauce.

| PREP TIME | COOK TIME | TOTAL TIME | SERVINGS |
|---|---|---|---|
| 25 Minutes | 15 Minutes | 40 Minutes | 3 |

## INGREDIENTS

- 3 tablespoons cornflour
- 350g thin-cut minute steak, thinly sliced into strips
- 4 tablespoons rice wine vinegar or white wine vinegar
- 2 teaspoons Chinese five-spice powder
- One red pepper, thinly sliced
- 100ml vegetable oil
- cooked noodles, to serve (optional)
- One red chili, thinly sliced
- Two garlic cloves crushed
- 2 tablespoons sweet chili sauce
- Four spring onions, sliced, green and white parts separated
- thumb-sized piece of ginger, cut into matchsticks
- 1 tablespoon soy sauce
- 2 tablespoons tomato ketchup
- prawn crackers, to serve (optional)

## INSTRUCTIONS

1. 350g of thinly sliced minute steak pieces should be combined with 3 tbsp cornflour and 2 tsp Chinese five-spice powder in a dish.
2. Heat 100ml of vegetable oil in a wok or sizable frying pan until hot. Add the beef, then fry until brown and crisp.
3. Scoop out the beef, then drain on kitchen paper. Pour away all but 1 tablespoon of oil.
4. One thinly sliced red pepper, one half of a thinly sliced red chili, the white ends of four spring onions, two smashed garlic cloves, and a piece of ginger the size of your thumb chopped into matchsticks should all be added to the wok. Stir-fry the garlic and ginger for three minutes to soften, but don't let it burn.
5. Mix the 4 tablespoons of rice wine vinegar or white wine vinegar, 2 tablespoons of sweet chili sauce, 1 tablespoon of soy sauce, and 2 tablespoons of tomato ketchup in a jug with 2 tablespoons of water, then pour over the veg.
6. Bubble for two minutes, add the beef back to the wok, then give it a good toss to coat.
7. Serve the beef on noodles, topped with the leftover ½ sliced red chili and the sliced green portions of the spring onions, if desired.

**NUTRITION: per serving**

• Fat: 23g  • Kcal: 454  • Protein: 26g  • Saturates: 5g  • Fibre: 2g  • Carbs: 32g  • Sugars: 15g  • Salt: 2.2g

## 4. STEAMED SEA BASS WITH BLACK BEAN SAUCE

This unique fish recipe makes an exquisite dinner for two, proving that Chinese food doesn't always have to be eaten from a takeaway carton.

| PREP TIME | COOK TIME | TOTAL TIME | SERVINGS |
|---|---|---|---|
| 20 Minutes | 10 Minutes | 30 Minutes | 2 |

## INGREDIENTS

- Cooked jasmine rice to serve
- 1 sea bass, head-on, gutted
- 2 tablespoons Shaohsing rice wine
- 2cm piece ginger, thinly sliced

### For the black bean sauce

- 2 garlic cloves
- 1 tablespoon groundnut oil
- 2 tablespoons fermented black beans, rinsed and crushed with the back of a spoon (you can also use 100g black bean sauce instead)
- 1 tablespoon Shaohsing rice wine
- 2 tablespoon grated ginger
- 3 tablespoons toasted sesame oil
- 3 tablespoons light soy sauce
- 1 small handful coriander, leaves picked
- 2 spring onions, shredded

## INSTRUCTIONS

1. Clean the fish in cold running water. Pat dry with kitchen paper, then cut three to four slits into the flesh on each side. Add salt and freshly ground white pepper all over. Place slices of ginger in the slits of the fish and inside the cavity.
2. The fish should be put on a platter that will fit inside your wok. Place an upside-down pudding dish in your wok and add water to come halfway up. Place the wok on the heat to bring the water to a boil.
3. Pour the rice wine over the fish, place the dish on the upside-down bowl, and cover the wok. Steam on high heat for nine minutes, then let it settle.
4. Make the black bean sauce while the fish is cooking. Add the groundnut oil to a frying pan or a hot wok. Add the beans, garlic, and ginger once it starts to smoke, or use 100g of pre-made black bean sauce and stir-fry for a few seconds. Add the rice wine, light soy sauce, and sesame oil, then bring to the bubble.

5. Carefully take the fish out (you can keep it on the plate you cooked it on). Serve with rice and garnish with coriander and spring onions. Drizzle with black bean sauce.

**NUTRITION: per serving**

• Fat: 29g   • Kcal: 511   • Protein: 49g   • Saturates: 5g   • Sugars: 8g   • Carbs: 11g   • Fibre: 1g   • Salt: 7.67g

## 5. PORK & CRAB 'ANTS CLIMBING TREES'

Make this delectable pork and crab snack from Sichuan; the name comes from the way the minced pork looks like ants climbing trees.

| PREP TIME | COOK TIME | TOTAL TIME | SERVINGS |
|---|---|---|---|
| 15 Minutes | 5 Minutes | 20 Minutes | 2 |

## INGREDIENTS

- 2 garlic cloves, finely chopped
- 2 tablespoons rapeseed oil
- 1 tablespoons oyster sauce
- 1 teaspoon dark soy sauce
- 1 tablespoons ginger, freshly grated
- 250g pork mince or minced rehydrated soy pieces
- 200ml hot vegetable stock
- 1 medium red chili, deseeded and finely chopped
- Two large spring onions ends trimmed, finely chopped
- 1 tablespoon shaoxing rice wine or dry sherry
- 1 teaspoon chili bean sauce
- 200g mung bean noodles, pre-soaked in hot water for 10 mins, then drained
- 150g crabmeat
- 1 teaspoon toasted sesame oil

## INSTRUCTIONS

1. Heat a wok over high heat, then add the rapeseed oil. Begin by stirring-frying the garlic, ginger, and red chili for a few seconds. Then add the pork mince and stir fry for three minutes until the meat is browned at the edges. Add sherry or rice wine, season with the black soy sauce and chili bean sauce and stir well. Add the hot stock and bring it to a bubble. Tip in the noodles and stir properly until all the noodles are well-coated in the sauce and have turned deep brown.
2. Add the crabmeat, give it a gentle toss, and add the roasted sesame oil seasoning. Add the spring onions, stir well, and serve right away.

**NUTRITION: Per serving**

• Fat: 14g   • Protein: 20g   • Kcal: 390   • Saturates: 3g   • Sugars: 1g   • Carbs: 45g   • Fibre: 1g   • Salt: 2g

# 6. CROSSING THE BRIDGE NOODLES

Enjoy this unique Chinese rice noodle soup. Ginger and other seasonings are added to a chicken and pork broth, then poured over noodles, vegetables, prawns, and shredded meat.

| PREP TIME | COOK TIME | TOTAL TIME | SERVINGS |
|---|---|---|---|
| 40 Minutes | 1 hr and 20 minutes | 2 Hours | 2 |

## INGREDIENTS

- Four chicken thighs, skin removed
- Four pork spareribs

## For the stock

- One thumb-sized piece ginger, peeled and sliced
- One star anise
- 4 spring onions, trimmed, chopped into 2.5cm slices
- 1 tablespoon Szechuan peppercorns
- 2 pinches of ground white pepper

## Accompaniments

- Four pieces of bean curd skin
- Two nests of cooked vermicelli rice noodles drizzled with toasted sesame oil
- Two large King Trumpet or King Oyster mushrooms, sliced lengthways
- Two spring onions, sliced on the angle
- 1 small handful of rehydrated Wood Ear mushroom strips
- Two red chilies, deseeded, finely sliced
- One Romaine lettuce, chopped into 2.5cm slices
- One shallot, peeled, finely sliced
- One large handful of baby spinach
- One small bunch of coriander, chopped
- Ten large cooked tiger prawns, deveined

## Condiments

- 2 tablespoons Chinkiang black rice vinegar
- 2 tablespoons freshly sliced chilies in 4 tbsp low-salt light soy sauce
- 1 tablespoon roasted ground Szechuan peppercorns
- 2 tablespoon hoisin sauce
- 1 tablespoon chili flakes mixed with 1 tbsp sea salt flakes
- 2 tablespoon chili garlic sauce

## INSTRUCTIONS

1. Bring 1 liter of water to a boil in a big stockpot. Add the chicken thighs and pork ribs, then simmer for 15 minutes while skimming any impurities.
2. Remove the water, then drain the meat. Clean the stockpot, refill it with 2 liters of water and add the meat. Add 2 pinches of salt and the ground white pepper, star anise, ginger, spring onions, and Szechuan peppercorns. Bring to a boil over medium heat, then simmer for one hour.
3. Prepare all the condiments by putting them in small dipping bowls.
4. Remove the chicken and ribs once the stock is ready, then shred the meat with two forks. Strain the stock, then discard the spices, ginger, and spring onions. Bring the stock to a boil.
5. Put the noodles on 2 large, wide plates. Garnish around the noodles with the mushrooms, bean curd skin, spring onions, Romaine lettuce, chilies, shallots, spinach, coriander, and tiger prawns. Shredded cooked meats should be added. Pour the hot stock over each bowl, covering all the ingredients.
6. Garnish with the condiments and add your preferred seasonings. Eat the noodles, and drink the soup broth at the end.

**NUTRITION: Per serving**

• Fat: 19g • Kcal: 665 • Fibre: 10g • Saturates: 6g • Protein: 57g • Carbs: 62g • Sugars: 13g • Salt: 14.5g

## 7. PRAWNS IN LONGJING TEA

Serve prawns with jasmine rice and Longjing tea's sweet, slightly bitter flavor as part of a Chinese feast to bring out their natural sweetness.

| PREP TIME | COOK TIME | TOTAL TIME | SERVINGS |
|---|---|---|---|
| 10 Minutes | 4 Minutes | 14 Minutes | 2 |

## INGREDIENTS

- 50g potato flour or cornflour
- One egg white
- ground white pepper, to taste
- groundnut oil for frying
- Eight large tiger prawns, shells off, deveined, rinsed, and drained

### For the Longjing tea 'stock.'

- 1 tablespoon groundnut oil
- 1 tablespoon Longjing tea leaves (also known as 'Dragon Well' tea)
- Two spring onions, whites only, sliced
- 1 teaspoon cornflour mixed with 2 tsp cold water
- 1 tablespoon dry sherry or shaoxing rice wine

# INSTRUCTIONS

1. Put the egg white and cornstarch or potato flour in a bowl. Whisk together to a fine batter. Mix in some sea salt and freshly ground white pepper to season. Add the prawns and evenly coat. Heat a wok less than half-full with groundnut oil, heat to 180C, checking with a cooking thermometer.
2. Lower the prawns into the oil using a spider strainer and cook for less than ten seconds. Drain and scoop out onto a platter covered in cooking paper.
3. Boil the kettle, place 1 tablespoon Longjing tea in a bowl, then pour over 150ml hot water. Steep it for 2 minutes.
4. In a different wok or large cooking pan, add 1 tablespoon of oil. Heat the oil over high heat until it begins to smoke slightly. Add 50ml of the tea and the prawns, followed by the shaoxing rice wine or dry sherry, spring onions, add a few tea leaf pieces and season with ground white pepper and salt, then stir in the cornflour mixture to thicken. If necessary, add a little more tea or water. Turn off the heat and serve with cooked jasmine rice and other Chinese dishes

## NUTRITION: Per serving

• Fat: 16g • Saturates: 3g • Kcal: 292 • Protein: 14g • Carbs: 22g • Fibre: 2g • Sugars: 1g • Salt: 1.6g

# 8. SALT AND PEPPER CHICKEN

Instead of ordering takeaway, make this quick, spicy salt and pepper chicken recipe at home. With a hint of Chinese five-spice, it is cooked with Asian greens in soy and honey.

| PREP TIME | COOK TIME | TOTAL TIME | SERVINGS |
|---|---|---|---|
| 10 Minutes | 15 Minutes | 25 Minutes | 2 |

# INGREDIENTS

- 1 teaspoon flaky sea salt
- 500g skinless, boneless chicken thighs
- 1 teaspoon Sichuan peppercorns (use normal peppercorns if you can't find these)
- 1 teaspoon Chinese five-spice powder
- 1 tablespoon cornflour
- 1 teaspoon sesame seeds
- 1 tablespoon honey
- 1 tablespoon olive oil
- 1 tablespoon soy sauce
- handful chopped coriander, sliced spring onions, cooked rice (to serve)
- 250g Asian greens such as pak choi

## INSTRUCTIONS

1.  Cut chicken thighs into strips. Crush the salt and peppercorns in a pestle and mortar; mix with the cornflour and five-spice; then, pour the mixture into a sandwich bag. Tip the chicken inside the bag and shake vigorously to cover the chicken with the flour mixture.
2.  Toss sesame seeds in a wok over medium heat, toast lightly for about a minute, then add olive oil. Add the chicken and cook for eight minutes until golden brown.
3.  Mix the honey, soy, and tip into the wok with the Asian greens. Cook for extra three minutes until it is well coated, and the greens are cooked.
4.  Serve with cooked rice and garnish with sliced spring onions and coriander.

**NUTRITION: per serving (3)**

• Fat: 9g  • Protein: 37g  • Kcal: 279  • Saturates: 2g  • Sugars: 7g  • Carbs: 12g  • Fibre: 2g  • Salt: 2.8g

## 9. STEAMED BASS WITH GARLIC & CHILI

Try this flavor-packed, low-fat fish dish, perfect as a mid-week meal. It's full of omega 3 and counts as 1 of your 5-a-day.

| PREP TIME | COOK TIME | TOTAL TIME | SERVINGS |
| --- | --- | --- | --- |
| 10 Minutes | 10 Minutes | 20 Minutes | 2 |

## INGREDIENTS

- 1 red or green chili, deseeded, finely chopped
- Two sea bass or other white fish fillets
- 1 teaspoon fresh root ginger
- 2 teaspoons sunflower oil
- 2 teaspoons low-salt soy sauce
- 1 teaspoon sesame oil
- 300g green cabbage, finely shredded
- Two garlic cloves, thinly sliced

## INSTRUCTIONS

1.  Sprinkle the fish with ginger, chili, and a little salt. Steam the cabbage for five minutes. Once the fish is cooked, place it on top of the cabbage and steam for 5 minutes.
2.  In the meantime, heat the oils in a wok, add garlic, then cook, stirring until lightly browned. Transfer the fish and cabbage to serving dishes, top with the garlicky oil, drizzle each with 1 teaspoon of soy sauce, and serve.

**NUTRITION: per serving**

• Kcal: 188  • Fat: 8g  • Saturates: 1g  • Carbs: 8g  • Sugars: 7g  • Fibre: 4g  • Protein: 23g  • Salt: 0.74g

## 10. SWEET & SOUR TOFU

Savor our sweet and sour tofu for one. It is vegan and healthy, with pineapple, onion, red pepper, and Chinese seasonings.

| PREP TIME | COOK TIME | TOTAL TIME | SERVINGS |
|---|---|---|---|
| 10 Minutes | 15 Minutes | 25 Minutes | 2 |

## INGREDIENTS

- 75g extra-firm tofu, cut into 2cm chunks
- 1 tablespoon rapeseed or vegetable oil
- 1 tablespoon low-salt ketchup
- ½ onion, cut into thin wedges
- One large garlic clove, finely sliced
- ½ red pepper, chopped into chunks
- 80g fresh pineapple chunks
- ½ tablespoon dark soy sauce
- sesame seeds to serve
- 1 tablespoon rice wine vinegar
- cooked basmati rice to serve

## INSTRUCTIONS

1. Heat half the oil in a wok over medium heat. Fry the tofu for 5 minutes, turning regularly, until golden brown on all sides. Transfer to a plate with a slotted spoon, and reserve.
2. The leftover oil in the wok should be heated. Fry the onion, garlic, and pepper for six minutes or until the vegetables soften. Add the pineapple, vinegar, soy sauce, ketchup, and 50ml water, then simmer for a minute or until slightly reduced. Stir the tofu back into the wok.
3. Cook the basmati rice following the instructions on the pack. Serve the tofu in bowls with the rice. Sprinkle sesame seeds.

**NUTRITION: Per serving**

• Fat: 17g  • Kcal: 530  • Sugars: 18g  • Saturates: 2g  • Protein: 15g  • Carbs: 75g  • Fibre: 8g  • Salt: 1.2g

# 11. KUNG PAO CAULIFLOWER & PRAWN STIR-FRY

Rustle up this cauliflower and prawn stir fry in twenty-five minutes. You can easily turn it vegan by leaving out the prawns and increasing the number of vegetables.

| PREP TIME | COOK TIME | TOTAL TIME | SERVINGS |
|-----------|-----------|------------|----------|
| 5 Minutes | 20 Minutes | 25 Minutes | 1 |

## INGREDIENTS

- 1 tablespoon vegetable oil
- ¼ cauliflower broken into florets
- Three spring onions, shredded
- 15g peanuts, roughly chopped
- One garlic clove, finely sliced
- thumb-sized piece of ginger, finely grated
- ½ red chili, finely sliced
- 60g raw king prawns
- 2 tablespoons hoisin sauce
- 1 tablespoon rice vinegar
- cooked brown rice to serve

## INSTRUCTIONS

1. Heat the grill to high. The cauliflower should be tossed with ½ tablespoon of the oil and grilled for 15 to 20 minutes or until it is soft and the sides are golden.
2. Once the cauliflower is cooked, heat the leftover oil in a small wok. Add the ginger, garlic, and chili, then cook for one minute. Increase the heat, then add the prawns and fry for a minute. Splash the hoisin and vinegar, let it bubble, then toss the cauliflower through the sticky sauce. Serve with rice and garnish with spring onions and peanuts.

**NUTRITION: Per serving**
• Fat: 20g • Kcal: 346 • Protein: 17g • Saturates: 2g • Fibre: 4g • Carbs: 23g • Sugars: 16g • Salt: 2g

## 12. CHINESE-STYLE KALE

You can give an old British favorite an Asian flavor with a few simple shakes of the right sauces.

| PREP TIME | COOK TIME | TOTAL TIME | SERVINGS |
|-----------|-----------|------------|----------|
| 5 Minutes | 10 Minutes | 25 Minutes | 2 |

## INGREDIENTS

- One large garlic clove, sliced
- 1 tablespoon vegetable oil
- 200g bag kale
- 1 tablespoon oyster sauce
- 1 tablespoon soy sauce

## INSTRUCTIONS

1. Heat the oil in a large wok, add the garlic, and cook for a few seconds. Add the kale and stir it around the pan to coat in the garlicky oil.
2. Add over 100 ml of boiling water, then cook for 7 minutes or until the kale has wilted and is thoroughly cooked.
3. Stir in the oyster and soy sauces and heat through to serve.

**NUTRITION: per serving**

• Kcal: 95 • Fat: 7g • Protein: 4g • Fibre: 3g • Carbs: 4g • Saturates: 1g • Salt: 2.26g • Sugars: 3g

## 13. CRISPY DUCK PANCAKES

Do not call the Chinese takeout for crispy duck with pancakes—our dish is much easier and healthy. Serve with a traditional plum sauce.

| PREP TIME | COOK TIME | TOTAL TIME | SERVINGS |
|-----------|-----------|------------|----------|
| 10 Minutes | 30 Minutes | 40 Minutes | 2 |

## INGREDIENTS

- Small bunch spring onions, shredded

- ½ cucumber, cut into thin matchsticks

## For the duck

- 1 tablespoon honey
- Two duck breasts (about 170g each)
- 1 teaspoon Chinese five-spice powder

## For the plum sauce

- 50ml agave syrup
- 5 plums, halved, stoned
- ½ teaspoon Chinese five-spice powder
- 1 tablespoon soy sauce

## For the pancakes

- rapeseed oil for brushing
- 150g plain flour

## INSTRUCTIONS

### The duck

1. Preheat oven to 160°F fan/180°C/gas 4. Mix five-spice and honey in a dish, then brush the duck. Move to a roasting tin and roast for 30 minutes until browned. Cool for ten minutes, shred the meat, and thinly slice the skin.

### Plum sauce

2. While the duck is heating, put all the ingredients for the plum sauce in a wok and simmer over medium heat for 15 minutes or until the sauce is thick and the plums are soft. Blend with a stick blender until it's smooth.

### Pancakes

3. Put the flour, 125ml boiling water, and a dash of salt in a dish and stir until a dough forms while the sauce is cooking. Knead for 5–10 minutes once it is safe to handle. Make 10 little balls out of it, then shape each one as thinly as possible. Each pancake should be fried in a frying pan for 20 seconds on each side or until cooked but not browned.

### To serve

4. Spread some plum sauce on a pancake. Add the shredded duck, a few cucumber slices, and a few spring onions.

**NUTRITION: Per serving**

• Fat: 18g  • Kcal: 402  • Saturates: 5g  • Fibre: 3g  • Protein: 13g  • Carbs: 44g  • Sugars: 19g  • Salt: 0.9g

# 14. CHINESE CHICKEN NOODLE SOUP WITH PEANUT SAUCE

Prepare an easy chicken noodle soup and liven it up with a spicy peanut sauce. It is low-calorie, with two of your 5-a-day. Ideal for busy weekdays.

| PREP TIME | COOK TIME | TOTAL TIME | SERVINGS |
|-----------|-----------|------------|----------|
| 15 Minutes | 30 Minutes | 45 Minutes | 2 |

## INGREDIENTS

- Four skinless, boneless chicken thighs
- 1 tablespoon sunflower oil
- One garlic clove, crushed
- 500ml chicken stock
- One thumb-sized piece of ginger, grated
- 150g straight-to-wok noodles (we used udon)
- 1 teaspoon soy sauce
- 150g mushrooms
- ½ hispi cabbage, finely sliced

### For the peanut sauce

- 1 teaspoon soy sauce
- 1 tablespoon peanut butter
- sriracha or other chili sauce (optional) to serve
- 1 teaspoon honey

## INSTRUCTIONS

1. Heat the oil in a wok over medium heat. Add the chicken and let it brown for about 2-3 minutes. Add the ginger and garlic and stir to coat the chicken. Fry for one more minute, then add the soy and chicken stock. Bring to a boil, then lower to a simmer. Cover with a lid and leave to bubble for thirty-minutes until the chicken is tender and pulls apart.
2. In the meantime, mix the sauce ingredients with some water. When the chicken is done, remove it with a slotted spoon and shred it on a platter using two forks. Add the cabbage, noodles, and mushrooms to the wok. Stir in the chicken, add a dash of sriracha, and ladle into bowls. Drizzle with the peanut sauce and serve.

**NUTRITION: per serving**
• Fat: 14g  • Sugars: 7g  • Saturates: 3g  • Kcal: 434 ·Protein: 48g  • Carbs: 25g ·Fibre: 6g  • Salt: 1.9g

## 15. QUICK & EASY HOT-AND-SOUR CHICKEN NOODLE SOUP

Keep tasting the broth and add as much rice vinegar and chili as you like to achieve the ideal flavor balance.

| PREP TIME | COOK TIME | TOTAL TIME | SERVINGS |
|---|---|---|---|
| 25 Minutes | 15 Minutes | 40 Minutes | 2 |

## INGREDIENTS

- 1 tablespoon groundnut oil
- 1 tablespoon Shaohsing rice wine
- 140g dried wholewheat noodles
- 2 tablespoons grated ginger
- Four skinless, boneless chicken thighs chopped into small chunks
- One medium red chili, deseeded, finely chopped
- 700ml hot vegetable stock
- 2 tablespoons rice vinegar
- 1 teaspoon dark soy sauce
- One handful beansprouts
- Four chestnut mushrooms, sliced
- 2 tablespoons light soy sauce
- 1 tablespoon cornflour mixed with 2 tablespoons cold water to make a slurry (runny paste)
- Two spring onions, sliced

## INSTRUCTIONS

1. Prepare the noodles in a small pan of boiling water as directed on the package. Drain, rinse with cool water to stop them from cooking further, then drizzle over a little oil to keep them from sticking to one another. Divide between two deep bowls.
2. Add the remaining oil to a wok heated over high heat. Add the ginger and chili when it smokes, and stir-fry for a few seconds. Add the chicken and stir-fry for two minutes as the meat changes color. Add the veggies stock, boil, then add the mushrooms—season with light soy, dark soy, and rice vinegar.
3. Bring back to a boil and add cornflour paste. Boil and stir until thickened. Stir in most spring onions and beansprouts, then ladle the soup over the noodles. Serve right away and garnish with the rest of the spring onions.

**NUTRITION: per serving**

• Protein: 42g • Kcal: 407 • Saturates: 3g • Fat: 12g • Carbs: 33g • Fibre: 5g • Sugars: 6g • Salt: 5.1g

# 16. MARINATED TOFU WITH PAK CHOI

You can intensify the flavors in your meal by marinating tofu in a mixture of ginger, soy, and chili. Serve with pak choi and rice for a satisfying fifteen-minute supper.

| PREP TIME | COOK TIME | TOTAL TIME | SERVINGS |
|---|---|---|---|
| 15 Minutes | 15 Minutes | 30 Minutes | 2 |

## INGREDIENTS

- 2 tablespoon groundnut oil
- 250g fresh firm tofu, drained
- 1cm piece ginger, sliced
- 1 tablespoon Shaohsing rice wine
- cooked jasmine rice to serve
- 200g pak choi, leaves separated
- 1 tablespoon rice vinegar
- ½ teaspoon dried chili flakes

### For the marinade

- 1 tablespoon grated ginger
- 1 teaspoon dark soy sauce
- 2 tablespoons light soy sauce
- 1 tablespoon brown sugar or golden syrup

## INSTRUCTIONS

1. Gently poke a few holes in the tofu with a toothpick to enable the marinade to seep in and enhance the flavor, then cut the tofu into bite-sized pieces.
2. Mix the marinade ingredients in a dish and add in the tofu chunks. Set aside for 10 to 15 minutes to marinade.
3. Heat a wok over high heat, then add half the groundnut oil. Once the oil begins to smoke, add the ginger slices and stir-fry for a few seconds. Add the pak choy leaves, then stir-fry for two minutes. Add a small splash of water to produce some steam and cook for two more minutes. Once the stems are cooked but still slightly crunchy and the leaves have wilted, season with salt, then transfer to a serving dish.
4. Give the wok a thorough cold-water rinse, reheat, and pour in the remaining oil. Add the tofu chunks while holding onto the marinade juice when it begins to smoke, and stir-fry for 5 to 10 minutes. Be careful not to break up the tofu as you toss it to ensure it is uniformly browned on all sides. Use rice vinegar and wine to season. The remaining marinade liquid should be added, brought to a boil, and reduced. Sprinkle the chili flakes and toss well. Spoon onto the pak choy and serve immediately with jasmine rice, if desired.

## NUTRITION: per serving

• Fat: 15g  • Kcal: 241  • Protein: 11g  • Saturates: 3g  • Sugars: 11g  • Carbs: 16g  • Fibre: 1g  • Salt: 3.47g

## 17. VEGGIE CHINESE PANCAKES

Skip the duck and serve these vegetarian pancakes with mushrooms, hoisin sauce, and greens.

| PREP TIME | COOK TIME | TOTAL TIME | SERVINGS |
|-----------|-----------|------------|----------|
| 5 Minutes | 15 Minutes | 20 Minutes | 2 |

## INGREDIENTS

- 2 tablespoons soy sauce
- 200g mushroom, sliced (we used chestnut)
- ½ teaspoon five-spice powder
- 4 tablespoons hoisin sauce
- ½ Little Gem lettuce, shredded
- ½ tablespoon sesame oil
- 1 tablespoon rice wine, preferably Shaohsing
- 1 teaspoon sugar
- Two spring onions, finely sliced
- Six Chinese pancakes
- 5cm length cucumber, deseeded, sliced into matchsticks

## INSTRUCTIONS

1. Heat a small wok. Add the mushrooms, five-spice, soy, rice wine, sugar, and sesame oil. Stir continuously until the mushrooms are cooked, the sauce is thick, bubbling, and clings to the mushrooms. You can heat or steam the pancakes to reheat them.
2. Serve the mushrooms, cucumber, spring onions, hoisin sauce, and lettuce in separate dishes, with the pancakes alongside.
3. Spread a pancake with a small amount of hoisin sauce to assemble. Add some mushrooms, cucumber, lettuce, and onions. Fold the pancake and enjoy.

**NUTRITION: per serving**

• Fat: 7g  • Saturates: 1g  • Sugars: 17g  • Fibre: 4g  • Kcal: 254  • Carbs: 37g  • Protein: 7g  • Salt: 4.1g

## 18. CHINESE SPICED DUCK SALAD

Who says a duck supper has to be pricey? With this flavor-packed salad, your meet will go further.

| PREP TIME | COOK TIME | TOTAL TIME | SERVINGS |
|---|---|---|---|
| 15 Minutes | 25 Minutes | 40 Minutes | 2 |

## INGREDIENTS

- 1 teaspoon Chinese five-spice powder
- 1 duck leg
- 1 carrot, cut into matchsticks
- 1 tablespoon soy sauce
- 140g rice noodles
- 1 celery stick, cut into matchsticks
- Two spring onions, sliced lengthways
- ½ cucumber, deseeded, cut into matchsticks
- 2 tablespoons hoisin sauce

## INSTRUCTIONS

Heat oven to 220C/200C fan/gas 7. Place the duck leg on a baking sheet, season it with five-spice, and roast for 25 minutes.

Cook the rice noodles as directed on the package. Drain and cool under running water, then drain well and toss with the celery, cucumber, spring onions, and carrot. Once the duck meat and crispy skin are cold enough to handle, separate them from the bone and shred them finely.

Mix the hoisin and soy sauce with 2 tablespoons of water to make the dressing. Divide the noodles into two plates, then top with the shredded duck. Drizzle the dressing over it and serve.

**NUTRITION: per serving**

• Fat: 15g • Fibre: 2g • Saturates: 4g • Kcal: 492 • Carbs: 69g • Protein: 25g • Sugars: 10g • Salt: 2.66g

## 19. HONEY & SOY DUCK SALAD

Use this rich mix of rocket and Chinese-style dressing to fix your salad dishes.

| PREP TIME | COOK TIME | TOTAL TIME | SERVINGS |
|---|---|---|---|
| 5 Minutes | 15 Minutes | 20 Minutes | 2 |

## INGREDIENTS

- 100g bag rocket & watercress salad
- Two duck breasts, skin on
- bunch spring onion, sliced diagonally
- 250g punnet cherry tomato, halved

### For the dressing

- 1 teaspoon fresh grated root ginger
- 3 tablespoons honey
- 1 garlic clove, grated
- 2 tablespoon soy sauce

## INSTRUCTIONS

1. Heat oven to fan 180C/200C/gas 6. Score the skin of the duck breasts, then season. Heat a wok over high heat, add the duck, skin-side down, and cook for four minutes or until the skin is crisp. Flip it over, quickly browns the underside, then move it to a baking tray.
2. Mix the dressing ingredients and spoon all but two tablespoons of it over the duck. If you want the duck to be pink, roast it for 10 minutes. Remove from the oven and leave it to rest for four minutes, then slice into strips. Mix the salad with the tomatoes, spring onions, and pieces of duck. Serve with the remaining dressing drizzled over the top.

**NUTRITION: per serving**

• Kcal: 558  • Protein: 34g  • Saturates: 10g  • Fat: 37g  • Sugars: 25g  • Fibre: 3g  • Carbs: 25g  • Salt: 3.12g

## 20. CRISPY CHILI BEEF

Ditch the takeaway and whip up this Chinese-inspired flash-fried steak with a sweet gingery sauce and red peppers.

| PREP TIME | COOK TIME | TOTAL TIME | SERVINGS |
|---|---|---|---|
| 25 Minutes | 15 Minutes | 40 Minutes | 3 |

## INGREDIENTS

- 3 tablespoons cornflour
- 350g thin-cut minute steak, thinly sliced into strips
- Four spring onions, sliced, white and green parts separated
- 2 teaspoons Chinese five-spice powder
- 1 red pepper, thinly sliced
- thumb-sized piece ginger, cut into matchsticks
- 100ml vegetable oil
- One red chili, thinly sliced
- Two garlic cloves crushed
- 1 tablespoon soy sauce
- 4 tablespoons white wine vinegar or rice wine vinegar
- 2 tablespoons sweet chili sauce
- cooked noodles, to serve (optional)
- 2 tablespoons tomato ketchup
- prawn crackers, to serve (optional)

## INSTRUCTIONS

1. Put 350g thin-cut minute steak strips in a bowl, then toss in 3 tablespoons cornflour and 2 teaspoons Chinese five-spice powder.
2. Heat 100ml of vegetable oil in a wok, then add the beef and fry until crisp and golden.
3. Scoop out the beef, then drain it on kitchen paper. Pour all but 1 tablespoon of the oil.
4. Add ½ thinly sliced red chili, 1 thinly sliced red pepper, sliced white ends of four spring onions, thumb-sized piece ginger (cut into matchsticks), and two crushed garlic cloves to the pan. Stir-fry for 3 minutes to soften, but don't let the ginger and garlic burn.
5. Mix the 4 tablespoons of white wine vinegar or rice wine vinegar, 1 tbsp of soy sauce, 2 tablespoons sweet chili sauce, and 2 tablespoons tomato ketchup in a jug with 2 tablespoons water, then pour over the veg.
6. Bubble for two minutes, add the beef back to the pan, and give it a good toss to coat.
7. Serve the beef on the noodles, topped with the remaining ½ sliced red chili, and sliced green portions of the spring onions, if desired.

## Nutrition: per serving

• Fat: 23g • Kcal: 454 • Saturates: 5g • Carbs: 32g • Fibre: 2g • Protein: 26g • Sugars: 15g • Salt: 2.2g

# THAI

## 1. TOM YUM SOUP WITH PRAWNS

Enjoy a delicious, nutritious, and simple-to-prepare homemade Thai tom yum soup that is vibrant, fresh, and flavorful.

| PREP TIME | COOK TIME | TOTAL TIME | SERVINGS |
|---|---|---|---|
| 10 Minutes | 30 Minutes | 40 Minutes | 2 |

## INGREDIENTS

- 150g tomatoes, roughly chopped
- 200g onions, roughly chopped
- 20g red chili, sliced
- Two lemongrass stalks, bashed
- 15g galangal, peeled, sliced
- 5 teaspoons fish sauce
- 70ml Thai coconut milk
- 5 teaspoons lime juice
- 270g whole raw king prawns, peeled, deveined, heads removed, reserved
- 120g oyster mushrooms, sliced
- One chicken stock cube
- 1 tablespoon Thai chili jam (optional)
- Eight lime leaves
- small handful of coriander, roughly chopped (optional)

## INSTRUCTIONS

1. Add 1.3 liters of water to a large wok over high heat. Add the chili, galangal, onion, tomato, prawn heads, lemongrass, and chicken stock cube. Stir, boil, lower heat to medium, and simmer for 20 minutes or until the liquid has reduced.
2. Strain the heated broth into a sizable heatproof bowl or jug, then discard the prawn heads. Put the strained vegetable and herb combination back in the wok and pour the broth. Stir through the lime leaves and mushrooms, then cook for three minutes until the mushrooms are tender.
3. Add 1 tablespoon of sugar, coconut milk, lime juice, the prawns, and the fish sauce. Bring to a boil and cook for 1-2 minutes until the prawns are cooked through. Remove from the heat. Remove the lemongrass and stir the Thai chili jam. Scatter over the coriander to finish and serve.

**NUTRITION: Per serving**

• Fat: 7g  • Kcal: 247  • Salt: 6.35g  • Saturates: 5g  • Fibre: 3g  • Carbs: 24g  • Sugars: 19g  • Protein: 20g

## 2. THAI CHICKEN AND SWEET POTATO SOUP

A vibrantly colored, smooth, spicy, and aroma-rich chicken soup with Asian flavors.

| PREP TIME | COOK TIME | TOTAL TIME | SERVINGS |
|---|---|---|---|
| 5 Minutes | 30 Minutes | 35 Minutes | 2 as a main or 4 as a starter |

## INGREDIENTS

- 2 garlic cloves, chopped
- 1 teaspoon olive or rapeseed oil
- 1 x 25g pack coriander, leaves, stalks chopped separately
- 2cm chunk root ginger, chopped
- One red chili, deseeded and chopped
- 500g sweet potato, peeled, roughly chopped
- One stalk lemongrass bashed
- 750ml chicken stock (made with two stock cubes)
- 2 tablespoons red Thai curry paste
- One small can (160ml) of coconut cream
- One lime, juice only
- Two skinless chicken breasts, sliced
- ½ teaspoon fish sauce
- 1 teaspoon sugar
- crusty bread, to serve (optional)

## INSTRUCTIONS

1. Heat the oil in a large wok. Add the chili, garlic, ginger, coriander stalks, lemongrass, and curry paste, and cook for three minutes until the aromas are released.
2. Add the chicken stock, sweet potatoes, and coconut cream, and cook for fifteen minutes or until the sweet potatoes are tender. Remove the lemongrass and discard. Transfer to a blender, then process until smooth. If freezing, freeze at this stage for the best results; if not, freeze the entire recipe as an easier alternative.
3. Return to the wok, add the chicken, and cook for five to ten minutes or until the chicken is cooked. Stir through the fish sauce, lime juice, and sugar, scatter with the coriander leaves, and serve.

### NUTRITION: per serving (4)

- Kcal: 360  • Fat: 18.1g  • Saturates: 12.4g  • Carbs: 30g  • Sugars: 10.8g  • Fibre: 3.2g  • Protein: 19.2g
- Salt: 2.1g

## 3. AUTHENTIC PAD THAI

Take the traditional pad Thai to new heights by adding king prawns, tofu, pickled turnips, and tamarind paste - a dish for two that's filled with flavor.

| PREP TIME | COOK TIME | SERVINGS |
|---|---|---|
| 15 Minutes | 10 Minutes | 2 |

## INGREDIENTS

- 2 tablespoons tamarind paste
- 1 tablespoon light brown soft sugar
- 200g dried flat rice noodles
- 3 tablespoons fish sauce
- pinch chili powder (optional)
- 1 lime, half juiced, half cut into wedges to serve
- 4 tablespoons sunflower oil
- 200g raw king prawns, butterflied
- 100g firm tofu, diced
- 100g beansprouts
- 2 tablespoons chopped pickled turnip (preserved radish)
- 100g salted roasted peanuts, chopped
- Two eggs
- Two spring onions, shredded
- soy sauce to serve

## INSTRUCTIONS

1. Soak the noodles in warm water for about twenty minutes, or until they are softened but still have plenty of bites, then drain. Combine the tamarind paste, lime juice, fish sauce, and sugar until the sugar dissolves. If you like your food spicy, add a pinch of chili powder. Can be made up to two weeks ahead and kept in the fridge. If you often prepare pad Thai, double the quantity and keep half.
2. Heat half the oil in a frying pan or a wok and cook the tofu on each side until golden. Prawns should be added and fried until they begin to turn pink. Add the noodles to the pan, then drizzle over the tamarind mixture with about 5 tablespoons of water. Stir together and cook over high heat until the noodles are cooked. If necessary, add a little extra water.
3. Once the sauce has been reduced, spread the beansprouts on top and fold them into the noodles. Push everything to one side of the pan, add the remaining oil on the empty side, and crack in the eggs. Fry for two minutes until the white is set and starts to crisp around the edges, then scramble the runny yolks in with the whites. Combine the noodles when the eggs have just been set.
4. Sprinkle over half of the peanuts, all the turnips, and half the spring onion, and quickly toss them together. Divide between two plates with the leftover peanuts, spring onion, chili powder, lime wedges, and soy sauce can be served on the side to garnish as desired.
5.

**NUTRITION: Per serving**

• Kcal: 992  • Protein: 45g  • Fibre: 6g  • Fat: 45g  • Carbs: 98g  • Saturates: 7g  • Sugars: 12g  • Salt: 7.5g

## 4. THAI-STYLE STEAMED FISH

Serve this Thai-styled steamed fish with Thai jasmine rice for a flavor-packed low-fat meal

| PREP TIME | COOK TIME | TOTAL TIME | SERVINGS |
|---|---|---|---|
| 10 Minutes | 15 Minutes | 25 Minutes – 30 Minutes | 2 |

## INGREDIENTS

- A small knob of fresh root ginger, peeled, chopped
- Two trout fillets, each weighing about 140g/5oz
- 2 tablespoons soy sauce
- One small garlic clove, chopped
- grated zest and juice of 1 lime
- One small red chili (not bird's eye), seeded, finely chopped
- Three baby pak choi, each quartered lengthways

## INSTRUCTIONS

1. Nestle the fish side by side on a big sheet of foil and spread the garlic, chili, ginger, and lime juice over them. Drizzle the lime juice on top and scatter the pieces of pak choi on top and around the fish. To make a package, pour the soy sauce on the pak choi and loosely seal the foil. Leave space at the top for the steam to circulate as the fish cooks.
2. Steam for fifteen minutes. (If you don't have a steamer, put the parcel on a heatproof plate over a pan of simmering water, cover it with a lid, and steam.)

**NUTRITION: per serving**

• Fat: 7g  • Saturates: 2g  • Kcal: 199  • Carbs: 4g  • Protein: 29g  • Sugars: 0g  • Fibre: 0g  • Salt: 3.25g

## 5. RED CURRY CHICKEN KEBABS

Kebabs and chicken are two of our most popular options so this former cover star is a winner - for barbecues or the grill

| PREP TIME | COOK TIME | TOTAL TIME | SERVINGS |
|-----------|-----------|------------|----------|
| 15 Minutes | 5 Minutes | 20 Minutes | 2 |

## INGREDIENTS

- 2 tablespoons Thai red curry paste
- Two boneless, skinless chicken breasts, cut into large chunks
- 2 tablespoons coconut milk
- One courgette, halved, cut into chunks
- One lime, halved, to serve
- One red pepper, deseeded, chopped into chunks
- One red onion, cut into large wedges

## INSTRUCTIONS

1. Heat a griddle pan to high or fire up the barbecue. Tip chicken, coconut milk, and curry paste into a bowl, then mix until the chicken is evenly coated. Thread chicken and vegetables onto skewers. Cook the skewers on the barbecue or griddle for eight minutes, often turning, until the chicken is cooked through and charred. Serve with salad, herby rice, and a lime half to squeeze over.

**NUTRITION: per serving**

• Fat: 8g  • Kcal: 251  • Salt: 0.85g  • Saturates: 3g  • Fibre: 2g  • Carbs: 10g  • Sugars: 8g  • Protein: 36g

## 6. THAI PRAWN, GINGER & SPRING ONION STIR-FRY

This stir-fry has a welcome spicy kick. The cooking process only takes ten minutes once the mixture has been made

| PREP TIME | COOK TIME | TOTAL TIME | SERVINGS |
|-----------|-----------|------------|----------|
| 30 Minutes | 10 Minutes | 40 Minutes | 2 |

## INGREDIENTS

- 1 green Thai chili, chopped
- 200g raw, peeled tiger prawns from a sustainable source
- 3 garlic cloves, 1 crushed, 2 finely sliced
- 1 tablespoon caster sugar
- 1 bunch coriander, leaves, stalks separated
- juice 1 lime
- 2 tablespoons groundnut oil
- 3 tablespoons fish sauce
- 100g beansprouts
- lime wedges to serve
- 1 tablespoon soy sauce
- 3cm piece ginger, finely sliced, shredded
- One red pepper, thinly sliced
- Eight spring onions, finely sliced
- 85g water chestnuts, sliced
- rice noodles or egg to serve

## INSTRUCTIONS

1. Put the prawns in a dish. Put the garlic, chili, coriander stalks (snip up using scissors first), and caster sugar in a small food processor or spice grinder and whizz together. Add the fish sauce and half of the lime juice, then pour the mixture over the prawns.
2. Heat 1 tbsp of oil in a wok, add the spring onions and ginger, and fry for a minute. Red pepper should be added and fried for one minute or until it softens. Water chestnuts and bean sprouts should be added and tossed together until the bean sprouts wilt. Add a good grind of black pepper and the soy sauce, then tip the lot into a serving dish.
3. Heat the remaining oil in the wok, add the prawns, lifting them out of their juices. Toss for two minutes until they turn pink, add the marinade and swirl the wok immediately. Tip the lot onto the vegetables. Sprinkle the remaining lime and snip the coriander leaves. Serves over noodles with more lime for squeezing over.

### NUTRITION: per serving

• Fat: 12g  • Kcal: 294  • Saturates: 2g  • Sugars: 17g  • Protein: 25g  • Carbs: 22g  • Fibre: 3g  • Salt: 6.32g

## 7. LEMONGRASS BEEF STEW WITH NOODLES

Get a taste of Southeast Asia with this flavorful, iron-rich stir-fry with chili, lemongrass, ginger, and coriander.

| PREP TIME | COOK TIME | TOTAL TIME | SERVINGS |
|---|---|---|---|
| 15 Minutes | 1 hr and 45 minutes | 2 Hrs | 2 |

## INGREDIENTS

- 2 garlic cloves, chopped
- 1 tablespoon of ginger, chopped
- 3 stalks lemongrass, outer leaves removed, finely chopped
- Two red chilies, thinly sliced (leave the seeds in if you like it spicy)
- 2 tablespoons of coriander leaves, plus an extra to serve
- 1 teaspoon of brown sugar
- 2 tablespoons of vegetable oil
- 2 tablespoons of dark soy sauce
- 250g stewing beef, cut into 2.5cm cubes
- 1 teaspoon of five-spice powder
- 100g wide rice noodle
- 400ml beef stock
- lime wedges to serve

## INSTRUCTIONS

1. Put the garlic, ginger, coriander, lemongrass, and 1 chili in a food processor, then pulse until puréed. Heat the oil in a wok over low heat. Add the purée and cook for five minutes. Stir in the soy, five-spice, beef, stock, and sugar. Put on a lid and boil, then reduce heat and simmer for one hour and fifteen minutes. Remove the lid, then cook for fifteen more minutes until the beef is tender.
2. Noodles should be prepared per the directions on the package just before serving. Drain thoroughly, then divide between two dishes over the beef stew. Serve sprinkled with the remaining coriander leaves and chili, with lime wedges for squeezing over.

**NUTRITION: per serving**

• Kcal: 502   • Fat: 20g   • Saturates: 5g   • Carbs: 43g   • Sugars: 4g   • Fibre: 1g   • Protein: 35g   • Salt: 3.5g

## 8. THAI CHICKEN CAKES WITH SWEET CHILI SAUCE

A light and nutritious supper is a great variation on the chicken theme. Serve with sweet chili sauce. Works well as a main course or a starter.

| TOTAL TIME | READY IN | SERVINGS |
|---|---|---|
| 25 minutes Minutes | 20-25 Minutes | 2-3 |

## INGREDIENTS

- One garlic clove, roughly chopped
- Two large boneless, skinless chicken breasts (about 175g), cubed
- lime wedges, shredded spring onion, sweet chili sauce, and red chili to serve
- small piece of fresh root ginger, peeled, roughly chopped
- 4 tablespoons fresh coriander, plus a few sprigs to garnish

- One small onion, roughly chopped
- 2 tablespoons olive oil
- 1 green chili, seeded, roughly chopped

## INSTRUCTIONS

1. Toss the chicken, ginger, onion, garlic, chili, and coriander into a food processor and season well. Blitz until everything is thoroughly combined, and the chicken is finely minced. Shape six small cakes with your hands.
2. Heat the oil in a pan, then fry the cakes over medium heat for about eight minutes, turning once. Serve hot with lime wedges, coriander, sweet chili sauce, red chili, and shredded spring onion.

**NUTRITION: per serving for two**

• Saturates: 2g  • Carbs: 4g  • Kcal: 306  • Fat: 13g  • Sugars: 0g  • Protein: 43g  • Fibre: 1g  • Salt: 0.28g

## 9. THAI-STYLE FISH BROTH WITH GREENS

A ramen-style noodle soup with sustainable pollock, healthy vegetables, and prawns - a low-calorie, low-fat bowl.

| PREP TIME | COOK TIME | TOTAL TIME | SERVINGS |
|---|---|---|---|
| 10 Minutes | 15 Minutes | 25 Minutes | 2 |

## INGREDIENTS

- 500ml chicken or fish stock
- 100g brown rice noodle
- 1 tablespoon Thai red curry paste
- 200g skinless sustainable white fish, such as Pollock
- Four lime leaves
- 1 tablespoon fish sauce
- 100g raw king prawn
- handful coriander leaves
- Two pak choi leaves separated

## INSTRUCTIONS

1. Prepare the noodles as directed on the pack. Refresh in cold water and drain well.
2. Put the stock in a saucepan and stir in the lime leaves, fish sauce, curry paste, and 250ml cold water. Bring to a simmer and cook for 5 minutes.
3. Cut the fish into roughly 3cm cubes, then add to the pan. Return to a simmer and cook for two minutes uncovered.

4. Stir in the noodles, pak choi, and prawns, and simmer for three minutes or until the prawns and fish are cooked. Serve in bowls scattered with coriander.

• Fat: 4g  • Saturates: 1g  • Kcal: 330  • Protein: 40g  • Carbs: 35g  • Fibre: 2g  • Sugars: 1g  • Salt: 2.9g

## 10. TILAPIA IN THAI SAUCE

Use this healthy white fish in place of cod, to prepare an easy one-pan meal.

| PREP TIME | COOK TIME | TOTAL TIME | SERVINGS |
|---|---|---|---|
| 20 Minutes | 10 Minutes | 30 Minutes | 2 |

## INGREDIENTS

- 2 tablespoons cornflour
- Four tilapia fillets
- 2 tablespoons soy sauce
- 2 tablespoons sunflower oil
- Two garlic cloves crushed
- Four spring onions, sliced
- small piece of fresh ginger, finely chopped
- 1 tablespoon brown sugar
- handful Thai basil leaves or coriander leaves
- One red chili, deseeded, sliced
- juice 1 lime, plus 1 lime chopped into wedges, to serve

## INSTRUCTIONS

1. Coat the fish fillets in the cornflour and set aside. Heat the oil in a wok, sizzle the fillets for three minutes on each side until crisp, then remove and keep warm. In the same wok, briefly fry the garlic, ginger, and spring onion, then add the soy sauce, lime juice, and brown sugar and simmer until slightly syrupy. Spoon the sauce over the fish, scatter with Thai basil, chili, or coriander, and serve with lime wedges.

• Kcal: 328  • Saturates: 2g  • Fat: 14g  • Carbs: 25g  • Fibre: 0g  • Sugars: 10g  • Salt: 2.94g  • Protein: 28g

# 11. THAI PRAWNS WITH PINEAPPLE & GREEN BEANS

This midweek stir-fry is packed with goodness from the crisp vegetables. It is flavored with Thai basil, lime, and ginger

| PREP TIME | COOK TIME | TOTAL TIME | SERVINGS |
|---|---|---|---|
| 10 Minutes | 15 Minutes | 25 Minutes | 2 |

## INGREDIENTS

- Two lemongrass stalks, tough outer leaves removed, the rest finely chopped
- 1 tablespoon vegetable oil
- thumb-sized piece ginger, shredded
- 100g green bean
- 200g raw king prawn
- 100g fresh pineapple chunks
- 100g whole cherry tomato
- small pack Thai basil leaves or regular basil leaves

### For the sauce

- 2 tablespoons liquid chicken stock
- 4 tablespoons lime juice, plus wedges to serve
- 1 tablespoon soft brown sugar
- 1 tablespoon fish sauce

## INSTRUCTIONS

1. Mix the ingredients for the sauce in a small bowl. Set aside.
2. Heat the oil in a large wok. Sauté the ginger and lemongrass until golden. Add the beans, cherry tomatoes, pineapples, and stir-fry for five minutes until the beans are cooked. Add the prawns and the sauce. Stir-fry for another five minutes until the prawns are cooked, then add most of the basil leaves. Serve with the remaining basil leaves and lime wedges scattered over.

**NUTRITION: per serving**

- Protein: 22g • Fat: 7g • Saturates: 1g • Kcal: 228 • Carbs: 20g • Saturates: 1g • Sugars: 18g • Fibre: 3g • Salt: 2.6g

## 12. THAI MUSSELS & PRAWNS

Give shellfish a Thai makeover with ginger, lemongrass, chili, coconut milk. Consider serving it as a fish course or starter when hosting a romantic dinner for two

| PREP TIME | COOK TIME | TOTAL TIME | SERVINGS |
|-----------|-----------|------------|----------|
| 10 Minutes | 10 Minutes | 20 Minutes | 2 |

## INGREDIENTS

- small pack coriander, leaves, stalks separated
- One red chili, chopped
- Two garlic cloves
- 1 x 400ml can coconut milk
- One thumb-sized piece ginger, peeled
- crusty bread to serve
- One lemongrass stalk
- 500g mussels, cleaned
- 200g raw king prawns
- One lime, cut into wedges

## INSTRUCTIONS

1. Blitz half the coriander stalks, garlic, red chili, coconut milk, and ginger in a blender.
2. Pour the coconut milk mixture into a saucepan, add the lemongrass, and cook over medium heat for five minutes.
3. Turn up the heat, add the mussels and prawns, then cover and cook for four minutes – the mussel shells should be open (discard any that haven't opened) and the prawns should be pink. Remove the lemongrass and discard.
4. Divide the broth and shellfish between 2 serving bowls and squeeze over some lime. Chop the coriander leaves and sprinkle the remaining chili over the top. Serve the broth with slices of crusty bread to soak it up.

**NUTRITION: Per serving**

• Kcal: 476  • Protein: 30g  • Saturates: 30g  • Fat: 36g  • Sugars: 4g  • Carbs: 8g  • Fibre: 2g  • Salt: 1.1g

## 13. THAI GREEN CURRY

Instead of purchasing a jar of readymade sauce, make a flavorful Thai green curry from scratch. This recipe makes more curry paste than needed; however, you can store the rest later.

| PREP TIME | COOK TIME | TOTAL TIME | SERVINGS |
|---|---|---|---|
| 20 Minutes | 25 Minutes | 45 Minutes | 2 |

## INGREDIENTS

- 2-3 tablespoons green curry paste (see below)
- 1 tablespoon vegetable oil
- 200g chicken thighs, skinned, de-boned, cut into chunks
- Two Thai aubergines
- 400g can coconut milk
- 50g pea aubergines
- 50g sugar snap peas
- 2-4 tablespoons fish sauce
- 2 baby corn, sliced at an angle
- 2-4 teaspoons sugar or palm sugar
- ¼ bunch of Thai basil
- Two lime leaves, stems removed
- One red chili, sliced

### For the green curry paste

- Eight green chilies, finely sliced
- Two garlic cloves, finely chopped
- 5g fresh turmeric root
- 25g galangal, finely chopped
- One lemongrass stalk, bruised, finely chopped
- Two stalks coriander root, finely chopped
- Four Thai shallots, peeled and thinly sliced
- Two lime leaves, roughly chopped
- ½ teaspoon shrimp paste
- 10g ginger, finely chopped (optional)

## INSTRUCTIONS

1. To create the curry paste, use a pestle and mortar to gradually mix all the ingredients—aside from the shrimp paste. Add the ingredients one at a time and pound them thoroughly after each addition to create a rough paste. Add the shrimp paste and keep pounding the ingredients until you have a smooth paste. The paste is done when you can no longer distinguish the ingredients. Will keep for 3-5 days in the fridge or up to three months in the freezer in an airtight container.

2.  Heat the oil in a wok over low heat to make the curry. Simply add the green curry paste and stir until fragrant. You won't need all of the green curry paste. Increase the heat to medium, then add the chicken pieces, coating them with the paste. When the chicken has browned, add half the coconut milk, while you avoid adding any water at the bottom of the tin – this will cause the curry to split. Stir constantly for 10 minutes or until the chicken is completely cooked and the sauce simmer.

3.  Add the remaining coconut milk, discard the water, turn the heat up to bring to the boil, then return the heat to medium.

4.  Add the baby corn and sugar snap peas, along with the Thai and pea aubergines, and simmer, stirring periodically, for about 10 minutes, or until the flavors combine, the sauce slightly thickens, and the veggies are soft.

5.  Fish sauce and palm sugar should be added gradually, stirring, and tasting after each addition until satisfied. Add the lime leaves and most Thai basil, then cook for 5 minutes to allow the flavors to blend. Pour the curry into individual serving plates and top with the remaining Thai basil leaves and sliced chili to serve.

**NUTRITION: Per serving**

• Kcal: 590  • Saturates: 31g  • Fat: 46g  • Salt: 4.1g  • Carbs: 16g  • Fibre: 4g  • Sugars: 11g  • Protein: 25g

## 14. EASY PAD THAI

Seemingly a national meal of Thailand, this version makes it simple to purchase and tastes incredibly genuine.

| TOTAL TIME | READY IN | SERVINGS |
| --- | --- | --- |
| 30 Minutes | 25-30 Minutes | 2 |

## INGREDIENTS

- 3 tablespoons lime juice, about two limes
- 125g (half a 250g pack) rice noodles
- ½ teaspoon cayenne pepper
- 2 tablespoons fish sauce (nam pla)
- 2 teaspoons light muscovado sugar
- 2 tablespoons vegetable oil
- Four spring onions, sliced
- 200g cooked, peeled tiger prawn, tails left on
- 140g beansprout
- a small handful of coriander leaves
- 25g salted peanut, finely chopped

## To serve

- sweet chili sauce
- One or two lime, cut into wedges

## INGREDIENTS

1. Put the noodles in a sizable heat-resistant bowl, cover with boiling water, and leave for four minutes. Drain, then rinse under cool running water.
2. Put the lime juice, sugar, cayenne, and fish sauce in a bowl and mix properly. Have all the other ingredients prepared by the cooker.
3. Heat the oil and fry the prawns until warmed. Add the noodles and spring onions and toss around. Add the lime juice mixture, and stir before adding the beansprouts, half of the peanuts, and coriander. Cook for a minute until heated through.
4. Serve with lime wedges and sweet chili sauce in a large dish, along with the remaining peanuts and coriander scattered on it.

**NUTRITION: per serving for two**

• Fibre: 2g   • Fat: 20g   • Kcal: 531   • Protein: 27g   • Carbs: 62g   • Saturates: 3g   • Sugars: 5g   • Salt: 3g

## 15. THAI BEEF WITH COCONUT DRESSING

Treat yourself to a rump steak. Cook it to your taste and serve it with jasmine rice and a fragrant, seasoned coconut cream sauce.

| PREP TIME | COOK TIME | TOTAL TIME | SERVINGS |
|---|---|---|---|
| 10 Minutes | 10 Minutes | 20 Minutes | 2 |

## INGREDIENTS

- 250g beef steak (we used rump)
- 2 tablespoons Thai green curry paste
- zest 1 lime, juice of ½
- 2 teaspoons vegetable oil
- 1 tablespoon soft brown sugar
- 160ml can coconut cream
- 2 tablespoons crispy onion from a pot (we used Danfood Onion Salad Crispies)
- One red chili, thinly sliced
- 300g pack cooked jasmine rice, or 100g rice, cooked, drained
- 200g pack green bean
- ½ small pack coriander leaves picked

## INSTRUCTIONS

1. Apply 1 tablespoon of the curry paste over the steak. Heat the oil in a wok and boil a small pan of water. Cook the steak for two minutes on each side for medium-rare or to your taste. To keep warm, transfer to a dish and cover with foil. Add the remaining curry paste, sugar, coconut cream, lime zest, chili, and juice to the pan and bubble until thickened. Add the beans to the boiling water, cook for 3 minutes, and drain.

2.   Pour any resting juice from the steak into the sauce and slice the steak into strips. Heat the rice to make it hot, then divide it between 2 bowls. Top with the steak, coconut dressing, beans, crispy onions, and coriander.

**NUTRITION: per serving**

• Kcal: 846  • Fat: 48g  • Saturates: 29g  • Carbs: 64g  • Sugars: 18g  • Fibre: 3g  • Protein: 36g  • Salt: 1g

## 16. 10-MINUTE PAD THAI

Who needs takeout when you can make a delectable meal in one pan?

| PREP TIME | COOK TIME | TOTAL TIME | SERVINGS |
|---|---|---|---|
| 5 Minutes | 5 Minutes | 10 Minutes | 2 |

## INGREDIENTS

- small pack coriander, stalks finely chopped, leaves roughly chopped
- 1 tablespoon of fish sauce
- 200g raw prawns
- 2 x 200g packs straight-to-wok pad Thai noodles
- One egg, beaten with a fork
- 85g beansprouts
- juice 1 lime, plus wedges to serve
- 1 tablespoon of roasted peanuts, roughly chopped, to serve
- 2 teaspoons of sugar

## INSTRUCTIONS

1.   Dry fry the coriander stalks and prawns in a wok for 1-2 minutes or until the prawns are pink. Add the noodles, egg, beansprouts, fish sauce, lime juice, and sugar. Use a set of tongs if necessary to quickly toss everything together for one minute more or until the egg is barely cooked and everything is thoroughly combined.
2.   After taking it off the heat, split it between two dishes and mix in most coriander leaves. Serve with lime wedges for squeezing over and scatter with the peanuts and remaining coriander.

**NUTRITION: per serving**

• Kcal: 494  • Protein: 37g  • Saturates: 2g  • Fat: 10g  • Carbs: 69g  • Fibre: 4g  • Sugars: 9g  • Salt: 2.91g

## 17. FRESH SALMON WITH THAI NOODLE SALAD

Prepare this nourishing salmon and noodle salad in under 20 minutes for a fast midweek meal. It is incredibly satisfying due to the balance of protein and carbs.

| PREP TIME | COOK TIME | TOTAL TIME | SERVINGS |
|---|---|---|---|
| 15 Minutes | 5 Minutes | 20 Minutes | 2 |

## INGREDIENTS

- 1 large orange, the juice, zest of half, the rest peeled and chopped
- Two skinless salmon fillets
- 125g French beans, trimmed and halved
- 75g frozen peas
- 50g mange tout, shredded
- 75g vermicelli rice noodles
- 1 teaspoon fish sauce
- 2 teaspoons red curry paste
- half a pack coriander or basil, chopped
- Three spring onions, finely chopped

## INSTRUCTIONS

1. Put a pan of water on to boil. Line a steamer with baking parchment, then add the salmon fillets, scattered with a little orange zest. Add the beans to the pan once the water is boiling, then put the steamer on top, and cook for five minutes. Take the salmon off, and set aside if it's cooked, but add the mange tout and peas to the pan and cook for one minute more, or for an extra minute if the salmon isn't quite done. Drain the vegetables, return the boiling water to the pan, add the noodles, then leave to soak for five minutes.
2. Put the fish sauce and curry paste in a salad bowl with a little of the remaining zest, the spring onions, and the orange juice. Drain and add to the salad bowl when the noodles are done cooking. Toss well, and add the basil or coriander, the chopped orange, and the cooked veggies. Add the fish juice, mix well, and serve in bowls with the salmon on top.

**NUTRITION: Per serving**

• Kcal: 517 • Saturates: 4g • Fat: 22g • Fibre: 8g • Carbs: 39g • Protein: 36g • Sugars: 7g • Salt: 0.86g

# 18. LEFTOVER ROAST CHICKEN PAD THAI

Want to make the most of your leftover roast chicken? All you need is pad Thai sauce and oodles of noodles to transform your chicken into something exciting

| PREP TIME | COOK TIME | TOTAL TIME | SERVINGS |
|---|---|---|---|
| 10 Minutes | 20 Minutes | 30 Minutes | 3 |

## INGREDIENTS

- 80ml vegetable oil or groundnut oil
- 150g flat rice noodles (2-3mm wide)
- Two garlic cloves, finely chopped
- 1 tablespoon shrimp paste
- small pack coriander, stalks, leaves separated, stalks finely chopped
- Three radishes, quartered
- 180g pack raw king prawns
- Four spring onions, shredded
- 150g leftover roast chicken
- 100g beansprouts
- Two large eggs
- lime wedges and chili flakes (optional) to serve
- 50g roasted peanuts, roughly chopped

## For the pad Thai sauce

- 2 tablespoons tamarind paste, thinned with 2 tablespoons water
- 80ml fish sauce
- 80g palm sugar
- ¼ teaspoon chili powder (optional)
- ½ tablespoon sriracha

## INSTRUCTIONS

1. Soak noodles in cool water for about thirty minutes or until al dente, then drain.
2. Meanwhile, make the sauce. Mix the fish sauce, palm sugar, tamarind, and sriracha in a small nonstick pan and heat the mixture just enough to melt the sugar. Taste it and add the chili powder if you prefer it hotter. Remove from the heat and set aside.
3. Add half the oil to a wok or a wide, high-sided frying pan heated over high heat. Add the garlic, shrimp paste, coriander stalks, spring onions, radishes, stir-fry for ten seconds, then add the noodles and 50ml water. Add the sauce to the noodles and stir-fry for an additional 8 to 10 minutes, or until the noodles are almost tender but still have some bite. A little more water can be added if the sauce starts to dry out.

4. Push the noodles to one side of the wok and add the remaining oil. Add the prawns and chicken, then stir-fry for about two minutes until the prawns change color. Push all ingredients in the wok to one side, crack in the eggs, breaking the yolks. When they settle on the bottom, scramble and mix through the noodles.

5. Add the coriander leaves, peanuts, and beansprouts. Serve with a sprinkle of chili flakes and lime wedges.

**NUTRITION: per serving**

• Kcal: 861  • Saturates: 9g  • Protein: 42g  • Fat: 43g  • Carbs: 74g  • Fibre: 4g  • Sugars: 29g  • Salt: 7.5g

## 19. PRAWN & COCONUT SOUP

This flavorful Thai green curry can be made quickly using only 4 ingredients. This simple prawn and coconut soup are ideal for a midweek meal.

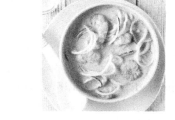

| COOK TIME | SERVINGS |
|---|---|
| 2 Minutes | 2 |

## INGREDIENTS

- 250g pack courgetti
- 400ml can coconut milk
- 3 tablespoons of Thai green curry paste
- 150g cooked prawns

## INSTRUCTIONS

1. One teaspoon of flavorless oil is heated to medium heat in a wok or a frying pan. Add the curry paste and cook for a minute. Pour the coconut milk in, let it boil for a few minutes, then add the courgetti and the prawns. Cook for a minute more to warm, then divide between bowls.

**NUTRITION: per serving**

• Kcal: 478  • Protein: 18g  • Saturates: 29g  • Carbs: 11g  • Fat: 39g  • Sugars: 7g  • Fibre: 4g  • Salt: 2.1g

## 20. THAI BEEF SALAD

A Thai chili dressing on a low-calorie salad and succulent rump steak. Put your spiralizer to use and treat yourself to a quick, flavorful supper.

| PREP TIME | COOK TIME | TOTAL TIME | SERVINGS |
|---|---|---|---|
| 30 Minutes | 5 Minutes | 35 Minutes | 2 |

## INGREDIENTS

- One rump steak (200-250g)
- One cucumber and one mooli, ends trimmed, halved widthways, spiralized into thin noodles, patted fry, and any long strands cut in half
- 2 teaspoons groundnut oil or sunflower oil
- small pack coriander, leaves picked
- 100g beansprouts

### For the dressing

- 1 tablespoon fish sauce
- One garlic clove, crushed
- One tablespoon soft brown sugar
- One red chili, finely chopped (deseeded if preferred)
- 1/2 lime, zested, juiced

## INGREDIENTS

1. To make the dressing, mix all the ingredients and stir until the sugar is dissolved. Toss the cucumber and mooli in a sizable bowl with half the dressing.
2. Apply the oil to the steak and season on both sides. Heat a wok until it is searing hot. Fry the steak for three minutes on each side for medium rare. Move to a plate to rest.
3. Pile the veggies onto plates, then mix with the coriander and beansprouts. Top with the steak and remaining dressing.

**NUTRITION: per serving**

• Kcal: 351  • Saturates: 5g  • Protein: 32g  • Fat: 16g  • Carbs: 18g  • Fibre: 3g  • Sugars: 16g  • Salt: 1.8g

# INDIA

## 1. BOMBAY POTATO FISHCAKES

Try an entertaining twist on traditional fishcakes by adding spices reminiscent of Bombay potatoes. Crushed poppadums are an inventive substitute for breadcrumbs.

| PREP TIME | COOK TIME | TOTAL TIME | SERVINGS |
|---|---|---|---|
| 5 Minutes | 20 Minutes | 25 Minutes | 2-4 (makes 6 fishcakes) |

## INGREDIENTS

- One frozen OR fresh flaky white fish fillet(about 200g; we used cod loin)
- Two medium potatoes, cut into chunks
- Four spring onions, sliced
- Two poppadums crushed or a handful of breadcrumbs (gluten-free if needed)
- 2 teaspoons of curry powder (gluten-free, if needed)
- salad, lemon wedges, and mango chutney to serve
- 2 tablespoons vegetable oil

## INSTRUCTIONS

1. The potatoes should be cooked for about 15 minutes in a pan of boiling water. Add the fish fillet to the pan for the last few minutes of cooking. Drain and leave to steam-dry for some minutes, then tip the fish and potatoes into a bowl with the spring onions. Use a fork to roughly crush the mixture together. Season, then mix in the curry powder. Shape the mixture into 6 patties. Put the crushed poppadums on a small plate and dip each fishcake on both sides to coat. To firm up the fishcakes, chill them for 30 minutes if you have the time. It will remain chilled for up to a day.
2. The fishcakes should be fried in a heated wok or frying pan over medium heat for five minutes on each side, until golden and pipinghot. Serve with mango chutney and salad on the side with lemon wedges for squeezing over.

**Nutrition: Per serving (4)**

• Kcal: 194  • Fat: 7g  • Saturates: 1g  • Carbs: 17g  • Sugars: 1g  • Fibre: 2g  • Protein: 14g  • Salt: 0.3g

## 2. SQUASH & CABBAGE SABZI

Serve this veggie Indian dish at an Indian feast. Made with cabbage, pumpkin, and spices, you can consume it as a main meal with roti or as a side dish with dhal and rice.

| PREP TIME | COOK TIME | TOTAL TIME | SERVINGS |
|---|---|---|---|
| 10 Minutes | 10 Minutes | 20 Minutes | 32 as a main or 4 as a side |

## INGREDIENTS

- 1 teaspoon nigella seeds
- 2 tablespoons sunflower oil
- thumb-sized piece ginger, grated
- 200g pumpkin or butternut squash, peeled, chopped into 1-2cm cubes
- Two garlic cloves, grated
- 200g cabbage, chopped (sweetheart or pointed cabbage works well)
- 1 teaspoon ground coriander
- 1 teaspoon turmeric
- 1 teaspoon ground cumin
- dhal, chutney, and roti or rice to serve (optional)
- 1 teaspoon chili flakes
- 2 teaspoons lime juice

## INSTRUCTIONS

1. Heat the oil in a wok and add the nigella seeds. Once they start to pop, add the garlic and ginger, and cook for one minute. Add the cabbage, spices, squash, and 1 teaspoon of salt, then mix everything with a splash of water, covering the wok with a lid. Leave to steam for eight minutes over low heat.
2. Afterwards, lift the lid to check if the squash is cooked. If not, rapidly replace the lid and cook the food for a few extra minutes. Add the lime juice, then check for seasoning before serving with chutney, dhal, and roti or rice, if you like.

**Nutrition: Per serving (4)**

• Kcal: 99  • Saturates: 1g  • Fat: 6g  • Carbs: 7g  • Protein: 2g  • Sugars: 4g  • Fibre: 3g  • Salt: 1.3g

## 3. GOAN PRAWN & COCONUT CURRY WITH CUMIN RICE

Quickly add some curry to your midweek meals by mixing spices with tomatoes, spinach, and shellfish.

| PREP TIME | COOK TIME | TOTAL TIME | SERVINGS |
|-----------|-----------|------------|----------|
| 15 Minutes | 15 Minutes | 30 Minutes | 2 |

## INGREDIENTS

- 1 onion, thinly sliced
- 1 tablespoon sunflower oil
- 1 tablespoon freshly grated ginger
- One red chili, deseeded, sliced
- Two garlic cloves crushed
- ½ teaspoon turmeric
- 1 teaspoon ground coriander
- ½ teaspoon chili powder
- 200g pack raw peeled prawn
- Ten curry leaves
- 400ml can half-fat coconut milk
- One large potato, diced
- handful baby spinach
- Eight cherry tomatoes, halved

### For the cumin rice

- 175g basmati rice
- 1 teaspoon cumin seed

## INSTRUCTIONS

1. Heat the oil and fry the garlic, onion, ginger, and chili for five minutes until starting to soften. Add the curry leaves, spices, and potato, then cook for one more minute. Stir in the tomatoes and coconut milk, cover, and leave to simmer for ten minutes until the potato is tender.
2. Add the prawns and spinach. Cook for one more minute until the prawns turn pink and the spinach wilts.
3. Meanwhile, make the rice. Put the cumin in a pan and toast for 30 seconds over dry heat. Add the rice, 400 ml of water, and salt to taste. Cover and cook for ten minutes until the rice is soft and the water has been absorbed. Serve with the curry.

**Nutrition: per serving**

• Fat: 22g  • Kcal: 771  • Saturates: 13g  • Protein: 33g  • Sugars: 9g  • Carbs: 105g  • Fibre: 6g  • Salt: 0.6g

## 4. INDIAN-SPICED FISH CAKES

Spice up leftover cooked salmon in these simple, freezer-safe fishcakes with refreshing raita.

| PREP TIME | COOK TIME | TOTAL TIME | SERVINGS |
|-----------|-----------|------------|----------|
| 20 Minutes | 6 Minutes | 26 Minutes | 2 |

## INGREDIENTS

- ½ teaspoon cumin seeds
- leftover avocado mayo, mango chutney, or raita to serve
- 600g potato, quartered if large
- Two spring onions, finely chopped
- 2 tablespoons chopped coriander
- plain flour for coating
- One egg, beaten
- 100g cooked leftover salmon, flaked into large pieces
- One red chili, deseeded, finely chopped
- 25g butter and 1 tablespoon sunflower oil

## INSTRUCTIONS

1. Boil the potatoes. In the meantime, briefly dry-fry the cumin seeds in a sizable nonstick frying pan. When the potatoes are tender, drain them, put them back in the pan, season well, then add the cumin, onions, chili, and coriander. Mash well. When cooled a little, beat in 2 tablespoons of the egg and gently fold in the salmon. Shape into four rough cakes, then coat in flour. If freezing, put the food on a baking sheet and let it freeze, then pack it up.
2. Melt the butter and oil in the frying pan. The cakes should be fried until browned, about 2 minutes per side. Serve with some raita or mango chutney, mayo, and some salad.

**NUTRITION: per serving**

• Kcal: 551 • Protein: 23g • Saturates: 9g • Fat: 26g • Carbs: 60g • Fibre: 4g • Sugars: 2g • Salt: 0.43g

## 5. SWEET & SOUR LENTIL DHAL WITH GRILLED AUBERGINE

Spice dinner with this superhealthy dish that serves as 4 of your 5-a-day, is high in fiber, is loaded with iron, and is reasonably priced.

| PREP TIME | COOK TIME | TOTAL TIME | SERVINGS |
|---|---|---|---|
| 10 Minutes | 25 Minutes | 35 Minutes | 2 |

## INGREDIENTS

- 1 teaspoon turmeric
- 100g red lentils, rinsed
- 1 tablespoon tamarind paste
- 3cm/1¼ inch piece ginger, grated
- 1 medium onion, thinly sliced
- 2 tablespoons vegetable oil
- 1 garlic clove, finely chopped
- 1 medium aubergine, cut into 2 cm slices
- 1 teaspoon curry powder
- lime or mango chutney, cooked basmati rice, and a few coriander leaves, to serve, if you like

## INSTRUCTIONS

1. Cover the turmeric, tamarind paste, and lentils with 500ml water. Add some salt, and boil for fifteen minutes or until very soft. Skim off any foam that forms on the top. In the meantime, prepare 1 tablespoon of oil and cook the garlic, ginger, and onion for about 5 minutes or until golden.
2. Add the curry powder and cook for two more minutes. Pour in the lentil mixture and cook for another ten minutes.
3. In the meantime, heat a griddle pan to high heat. Season the aubergine slices with the remaining oil. Cook until thoroughly done and browned, about 2-3 minutes per side. If desired, serve with basmati rice, lime or mango chutney, and a sprinkle of coriander.

**NUTRITION: per serving**

• Fat: 13g • Saturates: 1g • Protein: 15g • Kcal: 325 • Carbs: 41g • Fibre: 7g • Sugars: 10g • Salt: 0.72g

## 6. CURRY COCONUT FISH PARCELS

For a nutritious dinner, steam sustainable fish like tilapia in foil parcels with coconut, curry paste, and lime.

| PREP TIME | COOK TIME | TOTAL TIME | SERVINGS |
|-----------|-----------|------------|----------|
| 10 Minutes | 10-15 Minutes | 20-25 Minutes | 2 |

## INGREDIENTS

- 2 teaspoons yellow or red curry paste
- Two large tilapia fillets, about 125g/4½oz each
- 2 teaspoons desiccated coconut
- One red chili, sliced
- 1 teaspoon soy sauce
- zest and juice 1 lime, plus wedges to serve
- 140g basmati rice
- 200g cooked thin-stemmed broccoli to serve
- 2 tablespoons sweet chili sauce

## INSTRUCTIONS

1. Oven should be heated to 200°C/180°F/gas 6. Tear off 4 pieces of foil, double them up, and each should have a fish fillet in the middle. Spread the curry paste on top. Divide the lime zest, coconut, soy, and juice between each fillet. To make two sealed parcels, bring up the foil's sides and scrunch the sides and edges of the foil together.
2. Put the parcels on a baking tray and bake for fifteen minutes. Put the rice in a pan with a lot of water, cover, and simmer for 12 to 15 minutes until cooked. Drain properly. Serve the fish over the rice, and top with the chili sauce and sliced chili. Serve with lime wedges and broccoli.

**NUTRITION: per serving**

• Kcal: 438  • Saturates: 3g  • Protein: 28g  • Fat: 6g  • Carbs: 63g  • Fibre: 2g  • Sugars: 8g  • Salt: 1.3g

# 7. TANDOORI SPICED SEA BREAM

This Indian-inspired menu makes a memorable dinner for two and is easy to prepare.

| PREP TIME | COOK TIME | TOTAL TIME | SERVINGS |
|---|---|---|---|
| 20 Minutes | 10 Minutes | 30 Minutes | 2 |

## INGREDIENTS

- Two sea bream fillets
- drizzle olive oil for frying
- For the tandoori butter
- 1 teaspoon ginger paste
- 1 teaspoon garlic paste (blend lots of peeled garlic with a little vegetable oil, then freeze in ice cube trays)
- Two green chilies
- ½ teaspoon turmeric
- ¼ teaspoon red chili powder
- ½ teaspoon garam masala
- 100g unsalted butter
- juice ½ lime

## INSTRUCTIONS

1. In a small food processor or handheld blender, combine the ingredients for the tandoori butter plus some seasoning until smooth. Scrape onto cling film, and then shape it into a ball with the aid of the cling film. Twist the ends to seal in the butter, then chill until firm. The butter can be stored in the freezer for up to three months or the fridge for up to a week.
2. Heat a wok with a drizzle of oil until really hot. The fish should be seasoned, placed skin-side down in the pan, and fried for 4–5 minutes or until the skin is crisp and almost cooked. Carefully flip the fish over, then add a good tablespoon of tandoori butter as it melts. Serve immediately with the green beans and crushed saffron potatoes with coconut, with any pan juices drizzled over.

### Nutrition: per serving

• Kcal: 225   • Sugars: 0g   • Fibre: 0g   • Saturates: 5g   • Protein: 26g   • Fat: 13g   • Carbs: 0g   • Salt: 0.42g

# 8. INDIAN LAMB CUTLETS

This aromatic meal will have everyone's mouthwatering.

| PREP TIME | COOK TIME | TOTAL TIME | SERVINGS |
|---|---|---|---|
| 5 Minutes | 10 Minutes | 15 Minutes | 2 |

## INGREDIENTS

- 1 tablespoon curry powder (we used Schwartz Mild Curry Powder)
- 50g parmesan, finely grated
- 1 tablespoon olive oil
- Four lamb cutlets
- tomato chutney to serve

## INSTRUCTIONS

1. Heat oven to 200C/gas 6/fan 180C. Mix the curry powder and parmesan. Season the lamb, press the meat into the cheese mixture to coat. Heat the oil in a heavy baking tray or a wok, then fry the cutlets for two minutes on each side to brown.
2. Move to the oven for five minutes for medium or longer for well-done. Delicious when paired with some mash flavored with chopped coriander and a dollop of tomato chutney.

**NUTRITION: per serving**

• Kcal: 611 • Protein: 39g • Saturates: 24g • Fat: 50g • Carbs: 2g • Fibre: 2g • Salt: 0.81g • Sugars: 0g

# 9. SAMOSA CHAAT

Try this way of serving samosas for a heartier dinner. It is a tasty appetizer for dinner gatherings and special occasions like Holi.

| PREP TIME | COOK TIME | TOTAL TIME | SERVINGS |
|---|---|---|---|
| 10 Minutes | 20 Minutes | 30 Minutes | 2 |

## INGREDIENTS

- One large lemon, juiced
- One small red onion, finely sliced
- 2 tablespoons vegetable, rapeseed, or sunflower oil
- handful of fine sev or Bombay mix (optional)
- 400g can chickpeas, drained
- 1 teaspoon cumin seeds, plus a pinch for testing the oil
- ¾ teaspoon ground turmeric
- 1 ½ teaspoon ground cumin
- ½ teaspoon chili powder
- One teabag
- 200-300ml Greek yogurt, whisked
- Four vegetarian samosas (use shop-bought)
- 3-4 spring onions, finely chopped

## INSTRUCTIONS

1. Put the red onion slices in a heat-resistant bowl with just-boiled water. Leave for 10 minutes, drain, and mix with a little salt and lemon juice. Set aside. The onions will change to a gorgeous magenta color.
2. Heat the oil in a saucepan over medium heat to prepare the spiced chickpeas. To test it is ready, drop in a few cumin seeds – add the rest if they start to sizzle, followed by the drained chickpeas. Add turmeric, chili powder, ground cumin, 60 milliliter of water, and 1 teaspoon of salt. Break in the contents of the teabag and give it a stir. Cover, then simmer over low heat for about fifteen minutes or until all the flavors have been infused.
3. You may need to add more water as you gently crush some chickpeas in the pan to make the sauce.
4. The spiced legumes should be set on a serving plate. Samosas should be cut into pieces and layered on top. Drizzle over the yogurt, and top with the sliced pickled onions. Add the sev or Bombay mix and chopped spring onions on top.

**NUTRITION: Per serving (4)**

• Kcal: 366  • Protein: 11g  • Saturates: 5g  • Fat: 19g  • Carbs: 33g  • Fibre: 7g  • Sugars: 5g  • Salt: 2g

## 10. EGG CURRY

A delicious snack made with simple ingredients that tastes amazing when scooped up with naan bread.

| PREP TIME | SERVINGS |
|---|---|
| 10 Minutes | 2 |

## INGREDIENTS

- One onion, finely sliced
- Three eggs

- 1 tablespoon vegetable oil
- 175g green bean, trimmed and halved
- 2 tablespoons korma paste
- 175g young leaf spinach
- 100ml reduced-fat coconut milk
- 175g cherry tomato

## INSTRUCTIONS

1.  Eggs should be boiled for 8 minutes, then cool under cold running water, and then the shells should be peeled off. Fry the onion in the oil for about five minutes, or until softened and faintly colored, then stir in the beans and curry paste. Add 200ml of water and cook for 5 minutes while covered. Add the tomatoes, coconut milk, and spinach, then bring to a simmer, stirring until the spinach is wilted. Divide between two dishes, top with the halved eggs, and serve. Serve with pittas or toasted naan.

### NUTRITION: per serving

• Kcal: 351 • Salt: 1.38g • Saturates: 8g • Fat: 26g • Carbs: 14g • Fibre: 6g • Sugars: 10g • Protein: 18g

## 11. WEST INDIAN SPICED AUBERGINE CURRY

Make the most of aubergines with this vegan curry. You can serve it with roti or rice and it's low in fat but full of flavor.

| PREP TIME | COOK TIME | TOTAL TIME | SERVINGS |
|---|---|---|---|
| 30 Minutes | 15 Minutes | 45 Minutes | 2 |

## INGREDIENTS

- 1 teaspoon ground coriander
- 1 teaspoon ground cumin
- ½ teaspoon ground turmeric
- 2 tablespoons tomato purée
- One large aubergine
- ½ green chili, finely chopped
- 2 teaspoons caster sugar
- 1cm piece ginger, peeled, finely chopped
- natural yogurt or vegan alternative, cooked rice, lime wedges, and roti, to serve
- ½-1 tablespoon rapeseed oil
- ½ bunch of coriander, shredded
- Three spring onions, chopped

## INSTRUCTIONS

1.  Combine the dry spices with 1 teaspoon of salt in a bowl and put away.

2. Slice the aubergine into 1 cm rounds, and then use the tip of a sharp knife to score each round on both sides. Rub with the spice mixture until thoroughly coated, then move to a board. Fill the empty spice bowl with 150 ml of water and add the tomato purée, chili, sugar, and ginger. Set aside.

3. Heat the oil in a non-stick frying pan over medium heat, and arrange the aubergine in the pan, overlapping the rounds. Add the liquid mix from the bowl, boil, cover, then cook for twenty minutes, turning the aubergine periodically until it's cooked through. You might need to add up to 100ml more water if it seems dry to make it saucier. Season.

4. Serve the dish with yogurt, rice, roti, and lime slices for squeezing over. Sprinkle the spring onions and coriander on top.

**NUTRITION: Per serving**

• Kcal: 157  • Saturates: 1g  • Fat: 9g  • Carbs: 13g  • Fibre: 7g  • Protein: 4g  • Sugars: 12g  • Salt: 2.5g

## 12. INDIAN CHICKPEAS WITH POACHED EGGS

This fast, nutrient-dense veggie supper is filling and healthy. Chickpeas are a fantastic source of manganese, which is necessary for healthy bones.

| PREP TIME | COOK TIME | TOTAL TIME | SERVINGS |
|---|---|---|---|
| 5 Minutes | 10 Minutes | 15 Minutes | 2 |

## INGREDIENTS

- Two garlic cloves, chopped
- 1 tablespoon rapeseed oil
- 1 yellow pepper, deseeded, diced
- Four large eggs
- ½ bunch spring onions (about 5), tops and whites sliced but kept separate
- ½ - 1 red chili, deseeded, chopped
- 1 teaspoon cumin, plus a little extra to serve (optional)
- Three tomatoes, cut into wedges
- 1 teaspoon coriander
- ½ teaspoon turmeric
- ⅓ pack coriander, chopped
- ½ teaspoon reduced-salt bouillon powder
- 400g can chickpeas in water, drained but liquid reserved

## INSTRUCTIONS

1. Heat the oil in a non-stick frying pan or wok, add the pepper, chili, garlic, and the whites from the spring onions, fry for five minutes over medium-high heat. Set a large pan of water to simmer in the meantime.

2. Add the tomatoes, spices, chickpeas, and coriander to the sauté pan and cook for two more minutes. Stir in the bouillon powder, add enough chickpea juice to moisten everything, and leave to simmer.

3. Crack your eggs into the water once it has reached a rolling boil, poach for 2 minutes, and then remove with a slotted spoon. Stir the spring onion tops into the chickpeas, then lightly crush a few of the chickpeas with a potato masher or a fork. Place the chickpea mixture on a plate, top it with the eggs, and sprinkle with the leftover coriander. If desired, serve with an extra sprinkle of cumin.

**NUTRITION: per serving**

• Kcal: 412  • Saturates: 4g  • Fat: 20g  • Carbs: 27g  • Sugars: 8g  • Protein: 24g  • Fibre: 10g  • Salt: 0.3g

## 13. INDIAN SWEET POTATO & DHAL PIES

These small veggie pies IS an inexpensive weeknight dinner option. They are made with spiced red lentil dhal and topped with creamy sweet potato mash.

| PREP TIME | COOK TIME | TOTAL TIME | SERVINGS |
|---|---|---|---|
| 15 Minutes | 25 Minutes | 40 Minutes | 2 |

## INGREDIENTS

- One onion, halved and thinly sliced
- 650g sweet potatoes, peeled, cut into small chunks
- Two carrots, scrubbed, halved, sliced lengthways
- broccoli, to serve (optional)
- Two garlic cloves, finely grated
- 15g ginger, finely grated
- 2 teaspoons oil
- One vegetable stock cube
- 1 tablespoon curry powder
- 2 tablespoons tomato purée
- handful of coriander, chopped, plus sprigs to serve
- 85g red lentils
- generous spoonful 0% fat Greek-style yogurt

## INSTRUCTIONS

1. Cook the sweet potato in a pan of boiling water for fifteen minutes or until tender.
2. Heat the oil in a wok and add the carrot and onion for two minutes. Add the ginger and garlic, then cook, stirring for one more minute. Add the curry powder, stir round the pan, and add 750ml of the boiling water with the tomato purée, lentils, and stock cube. Boil for twenty minutes with the lid on or until they are tender and the juice has been absorbed. Stir in the chopped coriander.
3. When the sweet potatoes are cooked, drain and mash them along with the seasoning and yogurt.
4. Spoon the lentil mix into one or two separate dishes, then top with the sweet potato mix, scatter with the coriander, and serve with broccoli.

## 14. SOUTH INDIAN COCONUT & PRAWN CURRY

White fish and prawns provide a lot of energy in this low-calorie curry, which also has a flavorful blend of seasonings and a dash of creamed coconut.

| PREP TIME | COOK TIME | TOTAL TIME | SERVINGS |
|---|---|---|---|
| 15 Minutes | 25-30 Minutes | 40-45 Minutes | 2 |

## INGREDIENTS

- 0.5 thumb-sized piece ginger (no need to peel)
- One large onion, quartered
- Four garlic cloves
- 2 teaspoons rapeseed oil
- Four tomatoes, two halved, two cut into wedges
- ½ cinnamon stick
- Three cloves
- seeds from four cardamom pods, crushed
- ½ teaspoon black mustard seeds
- 1 teaspoon ground coriander
- ½ teaspoon ground turmeric
- 10 fresh or dried curry leaves
- 15g creamed coconut, chopped
- ½ fish stock cube
- One red chili, halved, deseeded, diced, or sliced
- 140g skinless cod, cut in half, halve again to make chunky strips
- 150g pack raw, shelled king prawns

## INSTRUCTIONS

1. To make a smooth purée, combine the tomato halves, onion, ginger, and garlic in a food processor with 50ml of water. You might need to scrape down the food processor's interior several times. Heat the oil in a wok, pour in the purée, cover with a lid, and cook for ten minutes. Add the half cinnamon stick, the cloves, cardamom, turmeric, mustard seeds, coriander, and curry leaves, and cook for some minutes, stirring. Add 300ml of water along with the stock cube, chili, and coconut, and boil for an additional 10 minutes. Taste to ensure the onion is completely cooked - if not, cook for another five minutes.
2. Lastly, add the fish, prawns, and tomato wedges, stir into the sauce, then cover and cook for five minutes. Serve alongside the spicy cauliflower pilau.

## 15. CHICKEN SATAY SALAD

Try this flavorful, no-fuss, midweek meal for high protein. Chicken breasts should be marinated, then drizzled with a punchy peanut satay sauce.

| PREP TIME | COOK TIME | TOTAL TIME | SERVINGS |
|---|---|---|---|
| 15 Minutes | 5-10 Minutes | 1hr 20 Minutes | 2 |

## INGREDIENTS

- 1 teaspoon medium curry powder
- 1 tablespoon tamari
- ¼ teaspoon ground cumin
- 1 teaspoon clear honey
- 1 garlic clove, finely grated
- 2 skinless chicken breast fillets (or use turkey breast)
- seeds from ½ pomegranate
- 1 tablespoon sweet chili sauce
- 1 tablespoon crunchy peanut butter (choose a sugar-free version with no palm oil, if possible)
- 1 tablespoon lime juice
- Two Little Gem lettuce hearts, cut into wedges
- sunflower oil for wiping the pan
- ¼ cucumber, halved, sliced
- coriander, chopped
- 1 banana shallot, halved, thinly sliced

## INSTRUCTIONS

1. Pour the tamari into a dish and stir in the cumin, garlic, honey, and curry powder. Blend thoroughly. Cut the chicken breasts in half horizontally to make a total of four fillets. Add the chicken to the marinade and thoroughly mix to coat. To enable the flavors to penetrate the chicken, refrigerate for at least one hour or overnight.
2. Meanwhile, mix the chili sauce with the peanut butter, lime juice, and 1 tablespoon of water to make a spoonable sauce. Wipe a wok with a little oil when it's ready to cook the chicken. Add the chicken, cover with a lid, then simmer over medium heat for five minutes, flipping the pieces over for the final minute until done but moist. Set aside, covered, to rest for some minutes.
3. Toss the lettuce wedges with the shallot, coriander, cucumber, and pomegranate while the chicken rests, then pile them onto plates. Add a little sauce on top. Slice the chicken, pile on the salad, then spoon over the remaining sauce. Consume while the chicken is still warm.

**NUTRITION: per serving**

• Fat: 10g • Saturates: 2g • Kcal: 353 • Carbs: 24g • Fibre: 7g • Sugars: 21g • Salt: 1.6g • Protein: 38g

## 16. SOUTH INDIAN COCONUT & PRAWN CURRY

This low-calorie curry has a lot of protein from prawns and white fish, a flavorful blend of spices, and a touch of creamed coconut.

| PREP TIME | COOK TIME | TOTAL TIME | SERVINGS |
|-----------|-----------|------------|----------|
| 15 Minutes | 25-30 Minutes | 40 Minutes | 2 |

## INGREDIENTS

- 0.5 thumb-sized piece ginger (you don't need to peel)
- One large onion, quartered
- Four garlic cloves
- 2 teaspoons rapeseed oil
- Four tomatoes, two halved, two cut into wedges
- ½ cinnamon stick
- Three cloves
- ½ teaspoon black mustard seeds
- seeds from four cardamom pods, crushed
- 140g skinless cod, cut in half, halve again to make chunky strips
- 1 teaspoon ground coriander
- ½ teaspoon ground turmeric
- 10 dried or fresh curry leaves
- ½ fish stock cube
- 1 red chili, halved, deseeded, diced, or sliced
- 15g creamed coconut, chopped
- 150g pack of raw, shelled king prawns

## INSTRUCTIONS

1. Put the ginger, garlic, onion, and halved tomatoes in a food processor with 50ml water and blitz to a smooth purée. You might need to clean the food processor's interior a few times. Heat the oil in a large wok, pour in the purée, then cover with a lid and cook for ten minutes.
2. Add the 1/2 cinnamon stick, cloves, mustard seeds, turmeric, cardamom, curry leaves, and coriander, and cook for a few minutes, stirring. Add 300ml of water with the stock cube, coconut, and chili, and simmer for 10 minutes. Taste to ensure the onion is fully cooked – if not, it's worth cooking for five more minutes.
3. Finally, add the prawns, fish, and tomato wedges, gently stir into the sauce, then cover and cook for five minutes. Serve with the Spicy cauliflower pilau.

**Nutrition: per serving**

• Fat: 11g  • Protein: 21g  • Kcal: 312  • Carbs: 19g  • Sugars: 13g  • Saturates: 5g  • Fibre: 6g  • Salt: 1.7g

## 17. MATAR PANEER

Serve this traditional vegetarian Indian recipe with cheese and peas in a hot tomato sauce as a quick midweek meal. Making it only requires 25 minutes.

| PREP TIME | COOK TIME | TOTAL TIME | SERVINGS |
|---|---|---|---|
| 15 Minutes | 10 Minutes | 25 Minutes | 2 |

## INGREDIENTS

- 225g paneer, cut into 3cm cubes
- 1 tablespoon sunflower oil
- 2.5cm piece ginger, grated
- 1 teaspoon ground coriander
- 1 teaspoon ground cumin
- Four large ripe tomatoes, peeled, chopped (or ½ 400g can chopped tomatoes)
- 1 teaspoon turmeric
- One green chili, finely sliced
- small pack coriander, roughly chopped
- 150g frozen peas
- naan bread, rice, or roti to serve
- 1 teaspoon garam masala

## INSTRUCTIONS

1. Heat the oil in a wok over high heat until it is shimmering hot. Add the paneer, then reduce the heat a little. Fry until it begins to brown at the edges, turn it over, and brown on each side – the paneer will brown quicker than you think, so do not walk away. Paneer should be taken out of the wok and drained on kitchen paper.
2. Put the cumin, turmeric, ginger, chili, and ground coriander in the wok, and fry everything for one minute. Add the tomatoes, mashing them with a spoon, simmer everything for five minutes until the sauce smells fragrant. If it is too thick, add a splash of water. Season well. Add the peas, simmer for two more minutes, stir in the paneer, and sprinkle the garam masala over. Divide into two bowls, and top with coriander leaves. Serve with naan bread, rice, or roti.

**Nutrition: Per serving**

• Kcal: 544  • Saturates: 18g  • Fat: 35g  • Carbs: 18g  • Fibre: 8g  • Protein: 35g  • Sugars: 14g  • Salt: 0.1g

## 18. LENTIL & SWEET POTATO CURRY

A storecupboard spice pot with red lentils, green chickpeas, and coriander. Serve with yogurt and naan bread.

| PREP TIME | COOK TIME | TOTAL TIME | SERVINGS |
|---|---|---|---|
| 10 Minutes | 25 Minutes | 35 Minutes | 2 |

## INGREDIENTS

- One red onion, chopped
- 2 tablespoons olive or vegetable oil
- 1 teaspoon cumin seeds
- 1 tablespoon medium curry powder
- 1 teaspoon mustard seeds (any colour)
- 100g green or red lentil or a mixture
- 500ml vegetable stock
- Two medium sweet potatoes, peeled, cut into chunks
- 400g can chopped tomato
- ¼ small pack coriander (optional)
- 400g can chickpea, drained
- naan bread and natural yogurt to serve

## INSTRUCTIONS

1. Heat 2 tablespoons olive or vegetable oil in a wok, add 1 chopped red onion, then cook for a few minutes until softened.
2. Add 1 teaspoon cumin seeds, 1 tablespoon medium curry powder, and 1 teaspoon mustard seeds and cook for one more minute, then stir in 100g green or red lentils (or a mix), two medium sweet potatoes, cut into chunks, a 400g can chopped tomatoes and 500ml vegetable stock.
3. Bring to a boil, cover, and simmer for twenty minutes until the sweet potatoes and lentils are tender. Add a drained 400g can of chickpeas, and heat through.
4. If you prefer, season and sprinkle with ¼ small pack coriander. Serve with seasoned yogurt and naan bread.

**Nutrition: per serving**

• Fat: 18g  • Saturates: 2g  • Kcal: 613  • Carbs: 91g  • Protein: 27g  • Sugars: 21g  • Fibre: 16g  • Salt: 1.8g

## 19. SOUTH INDIAN FISH CURRY WITH CHICKPEAS

This recipe gives a satisfying, spicy supper with brain-boosting properties.

| PREP TIME | COOK TIME | TOTAL TIME | SERVINGS |
|-----------|-----------|------------|----------|
| 10 Minutes | 25 Minutes | 35 Minutes | 2 |

## INGREDIENTS

- One onion, halved, sliced
- 1 teaspoon rapeseed oil
- 1 teaspoon ground turmeric
- ½ teaspoon cumin seed
- 1 teaspoon black mustard seeds
- ¼ teaspoon ground fenugreek
- ½ thumb-sized piece ginger, finely chopped
- ¼ teaspoon chili flakes
- One large garlic clove, finely grated
- 210g can chickpea, drained
- 400g can chopped tomato
- ½ fish stock cube, crumbled
- 350g fresh mackerel, cut into thick pieces (or use boneless fillets)
- 2 tablespoons tamarind paste (optional)

### To serve

- small bunch coriander, chopped
- 25g flaked almond
- 250g pack cooked brown rice

## INSTRUCTIONS

1. Heat the oil in a wok. Add the onion, cover, and cook for 5 minutes, occasionally stirring, until golden. Add the whole and ground spices, garlic, and ginger, stir for about thirty seconds to release their flavors, and pour in a can of water, tomatoes, stock cube, and chickpeas. Cover and leave to cook for 20 mins.
2. Add the mackerel, stir in the tamarind (if using), then cover and cook for an additional 8 minutes. Rice should be cooked according to the pack's instructions, then tip into a bowl, and toss with the coriander and almonds. Serve with the curry.

**NUTRITION: per serving**

• Fat: 33g  • Protein: 41g  • Saturates: 6g  • Kcal: 535  • Carbs: 22g  • Fibre: 7g  • Salt: 0.9g  • Sugars: 10g

# 20. PRAWN CURRY IN A HURRY

Minimum shopping, maximum taste. If Indian food isn't your style, make this Thai prawn curry with an easy switch.

| PREP TIME | COOK TIME | TOTAL TIME | SERVINGS |
|---|---|---|---|
| 5 Minutes | 10 Minutes | 15 Minutes | 2 |

## INGREDIENTS

- One onion, finely sliced
- 2 tablespoons curry paste (we used Patak's Origional Balti curry paste)
- 200g large cooked or raw prawns, defrosted if frozen
- large bunch coriander, leaves, stalks chopped
- 400g can chopped tomatoes with garlic

## INSTRUCTIONS

1. Add a little oil from the curry paste jar into a wok, slowly heat, then add the onion. Sizzle over low heat for four minutes until the onion's tenders, then stir in the paste and cook for a few minutes longer. Stir in the tomatoes and prawns, then bring to a boil. If using raw prawns, simmer until they are fully cooked and have changed color. If you prefer, add the coriander before serving with naan bread and boiled rice.

**NUTRITION: per serving**

• Kcal: 166  • Saturates: 1g  • Fat: 4g  • Carbs: 11g  • Protein: 22g  • Fibre: 3g  • Sugars: 8g  • Salt: 1.08g

# KOREAN

## 1. SPICY KIMCHI PANCAKE (KIMCHI JEON)

Make these spicy pancakes with kimchi (sour cabbage) and gochujang (Korean red pepper paste) for a taste of Korea. They are packed with flavor.

| PREP TIME | COOK TIME | TOTAL TIME | SERVINGS |
|---|---|---|---|
| 10 Minutes | 10 Minutes | 20 Minutes | 2 |

## INGREDIENTS

- 1 tablespoon corn flour
- 2 spring onions, finely sliced
- 175g self-rising flour
- 2 teaspoons gochujang (Korean red pepper paste), or use half miso paste, half sriracha
- 200g vegan fermented (sour) kimchi, drained, finely chopped, and 2 tablespoons liquid reserved
- 6 tablespoons vegetable oil

## INSTRUCTIONS

Place the flours in a bowl and add 200ml of ice-cold water and the reserved kimchi liquid. Whisk until a smooth batter is formed.

Mix the gochujang, spring onions, and kimchi; the batter should be a thick pancake, like a drop scone consistency. If you feel like it needs a little thickening, you can add a tbsp of flour.

Place a large non-stick wok over high heat with 2 tablespoons of vegetable oil. Ladle the pancake mixture into the pan. Utilize the back of the ladle to smoothen the mix out to create a thin, even layer. Reduce the heat to medium-high. Fry for two to three minutes or until the sides begin to crisp and air bubbles pop on the surface.

Flip the pancake, then slightly lift the side of the pancake with a spatula and add another tbsp of oil should be added below. Shake the pan a little to ensure that the oil covers the entire bottom of the pancake.

To ensure the pancake is crispy, use a spatula to press on top of the pancake. Fry for two more minutes.

One final flip, apply pressure on the pancake once more and fry for thirty seconds. Drain on kitchen paper and keeps heated in a low oven while you cook the second pancake similarly. Serve (optionally sliced into bite-sized pieces)

## NUTRITION: Per serving

• Fat: 35g  • Carbs: 82g  • Protein: 10g  • Sugars: 4g  • Saturates: 3g  • Kcal: 692  • Fibre: 6g  • Salt: 3.42g

## 2. STIR-FRIED KOREAN BEEF

Whip up a speedy beef, spinach and beansprout stir-fry seasoned with sweet mirin, sesame seeds, soy sauce, and garlic.

| PREP TIME | COOK TIME | TOTAL TIME | SERVINGS |
|---|---|---|---|
| 10 Minutes | 10 Minutes | 20 Minutes | 2 |

## INGREDIENTS

- 1 tablespoon mirin or clear honey
- 1 tablespoon soy sauce
- handful sesame seeds, toasted
- 2 teaspoons corn flour, mixed to a paste with 2 tablespoons water
- 300g beef frying steak, thinly sliced
- 1 tablespoon vegetable oil
- 1 garlic clove, thinly sliced
- Three spring onions, sliced into small pieces
- 1One red chili, finely chopped
- 300g pack beansprout
- cooked rice, to serve (optional)
- 100g bag baby spinach

## INSTRUCTIONS

1. Mix the mirin or honey, soy, and cornflour paste in a small bowl. Heat the oil in a wok. Season the beef, sear in batches, remove to a plate, then cover with foil to keep warm. Fry the chili and garlic, then add the beansprouts and spring onions, and stir-fry for two minutes.
2. Return the beef to the wok and add the spinach with the sauce. Keep stir-frying for three more minutes until the spinach has wilted. If desired, serve with some rice and sesame seeds spread on top.

**NUTRITION: per serving**

• Protein: 40g  • Fat: 27g  • Saturates: 8g  • Kcal: 470  • Carbs: 17g  • Fibre: 6g  • Sugars: 5g  • Salt: 1.8g

## 3. EASY BIBIMBAP

A Korean rice bowl packed with goodies - fried egg, sliced steak, carrot, spinach, and toasted sesame seeds, plus sriracha or gochujang for a chili kick.

| PREP TIME | COOK TIME | TOTAL TIME | SERVINGS |
|-----------|-----------|------------|----------|
| 20 Minutes | 15 Minutes | 35 Minutes | 2 |

## INGREDIENTS

- 2 teaspoons light soy sauce, plus extra to serve
- 100g thin beef steak
- 120g rice
- 50g spinach
- sunflower oil
- ½ teaspoon toasted sesame seeds
- 1 carrot, cut into matchsticks
- Two eggs
- a thumb-sized piece of fresh root ginger, peeled, cut into fine matchsticks

### Sauce

- 2 teaspoons toasted sesame seeds
- 4 teaspoons light soy sauce
- 2 tablespoons gochujang or 4 teaspoons sriracha and 2 teaspoons white miso paste
- 2 teaspoons cider vinegar

## INSTRUCTIONS

1. Put the steak into a bowl, then add the soy sauce.
2. Boil the rice as directed on the package. In the meantime, heat 1 teaspoon of oil in a wok. Add the steak, leaving the soy sauce in the bowl. Fry immediately at a high temperature until well browned on the outside, put it on a board, then cover it with foil to rest. In the same wok, stir-fry the carrots for 2 to 3 minutes or until they soften, then transfer them to a dish. After that, add the spinach and continue to fry until it barely wilts (about a minute). Lastly, fry the eggs, adding a little oil if the wok is dry.
3. When the rice is ready, drain and pile it into two bowls. Slice the steak and put it on top of the rice. Add a clump of the cooked carrots, the spinach, and, lastly, the ginger. Sprinkle the sesame seeds on top. Stir the sauce ingredients in a bowl and serve alongside the rice. The best way to consume it is to dollop on a good amount of sauce, crack open an egg, and then combine everything so that the sauce and runny egg yolk are delightfully combined with the steak and veggies.

**NUTRITION: per serving**

• Fat: 17g  • Saturates: 4g  • Kcal: 494  • Carbs: 57g  • Protein: 27g  • Sugars: 8g  • Fibre: 3g  • Salt: 2.4g

# 4. JAPCHAE (STIR FRIED NOODLES)

Make a traditional Korean dish by combining sweet potato noodles, chestnut mushrooms, tender steak strips, and spinach in a savory sauce.

| PREP TIME | COOK TIME | TOTAL TIME | SERVINGS |
|-----------|-----------|------------|----------|
| 20 Minutes | 20 Minutes | 40 Minutes | 2 as a main – 4 as a side |

## INGREDIENTS

- vegetable oil, for frying
- 150g dangmyun (sweet potato noodles)
- One egg
- 100g frying steak, cut into 5mm strips
- One red pepper, thinly sliced
- ½ carrot, sliced into matchsticks
- 100g chestnut mushrooms, thinly sliced
- sesame seeds, to garnish
- Three spring onions, cut into 5cm lengths

## For the japchae sauce

- 4 tablespoons dark soy sauce
- 1 tablespoons sesame oil
- 2 teaspoons caster sugar
- 1 small garlic clove, finely grated
- 2 tablespoons toasted sesame seeds (with some extra for garnish)
- ½ teaspoon finely ground white pepper

## For the beef marinade

- Two small garlic cloves, finely grated
- 1 tablespoon soy sauce
- 2 teaspoons caster sugar

## For the spinach

- ¼ teaspoon salt
- 200g spinach
- 1 small garlic clove, finely grated
- 2 teaspoons toasted sesame seeds
- ½ teaspoon sesame oil

## INSTRUCTIONS

1. Cook the noodles according to the instruction on the package, then drain and rinse under cool water. The ingredients for the japchae sauce should be mixed and set aside.

2. Combine the beef marinade ingredients with ½ teaspoon of ground black pepper. Tip the beef into the marinade and make sure everything is properly mixed. Set aside for ten minutes to marinate.

3. Put the spinach in a sizable heat-resistant bowl, then boil it. Wilt for a minute. Spinach should be drained and washed under cool water. Remove any extra water by squeezing. In a bowl, combine the drained spinach with the remaining ingredients and ¼ teaspoon of salt and mix. Set to one side.

4. Crack the egg into a bowl and stir with a fork. Heat the vegetable oil in a wok over medium heat. Add the egg and a pinch of salt, then move the wok to coat it with a thin layer of egg. Fry for thirty seconds, flip, and cook on the second side for thirty seconds to create a thin omelet. Remove from the wok to cool and roll into a tube form to facilitate slicing. Egg should be thinly sliced, about 0.5cm thick. Set aside.

5. Heat 1 tablespoon vegetable oil over medium heat in a large wok. Place the beef in the wok using a set of tongs, and fry for 1-2 minutes. Remove the beef and set aside. Wipe the wok clean using kitchen paper and add 1 teaspoon more oil. Tip in the carrots with a pinch of salt and fry for two minutes until slightly softened. Remove from the wok, wipe with a paper towel, and add another tbsp of oil. Fry the peppers for two to three minutes until tender; remove from the wok, wipe it clean, and add another tbsp of oil before frying the mushrooms for seven minutes until soft and golden.

6. Wipe out the wok and keep it on medium heat. Pour in 2 tablespoons vegetable oil and add the noodles to the wok when hot and toss with a pair of tongs for two minutes to heat through. Once the noodles are heated, pour the japchae sauce, and all the other prepped ingredients, including the spring onions. Toss the ingredients over high heat for two more minutes, ensuring everything is well mixed and coated with the sauce. Serve right away with some sesame seeds on top.

**NUTRITION: Per serving**

• Protein: 15g  • Fat: 30g  • Saturates: 4g  • Kcal: 503  • Carbs: 41g  • Fibre: 3g  • Sugars: 10g  • Salt: 3.05g

## 5. KOREAN-STYLE PRAWN & SPRING ONION PANCAKE

This savory pancake in the Korean style cooks in just 20 minutes, making it an easy-to-prepare meal for one.

| PREP TIME | COOK TIME | TOTAL TIME | SERVINGS |
|---|---|---|---|
| 10 Minutes | 10 Minutes | 20 Minutes | 1 |

## INGREDIENTS

- pinch of chili powder
- 75g plain flour
- 100g small cooked prawns
- One egg
- 1 tablespoon oil

- One garlic clove, crushed
- Four spring onions, trimmed, shredded lengthways

## For the dipping sauce

- 1 tablespoon soy sauce
- 2 tablespoons rice vinegar
- pinch of sugar
- One red chili, finely chopped

## INSTRUCTIONS

The dipping sauce ingredients should be combined, then set aside.

Mix the flour, chili powder, and a pinch of salt in a bowl. Beat together 100ml water, the garlic, and the egg. Make a well in the center of the flour, and pour in the water mix, beating all the time to make a smooth batter.

Heat the oil in a medium non-stick wok and cook the spring onions for one minute until softening. Sprinkle the prawns on top, then pour on the batter to cover. Cook for 3 to 4 minutes on medium heat or until the top starts to set and the bottom is completely set and turning golden. Flip over and cook the other side for three mins more until cooked. Slice into wedges. Serve with the dipping sauce.

| NUTRITION: per serving |
|---|

• Protein: 31g  • Fat: 21g  • Kcal: 545  • Saturates: 4g  • Fibre: 4g  • Carbs: 59g  • Sugars: 4g  • Salt: 3g

## 6. KOREAN SESAME PORK STIR-FRY

Throw in strips of pork loin into a wok, sesame seeds, and crunchy veg for a quick, satisfying meal that's done in 30 minutes.

| PREP TIME | COOK TIME | TOTAL TIME | SERVINGS |
|---|---|---|---|
| 15 Minutes | 15 Minutes | 30 Minutes | 3 |

## INGREDIENTS

- 25g sesame seeds
- 2 tablespoons sesame oil
- 2 red peppers, deseeded, thinly sliced
- 1 tablespoon soy sauce
- 2 tablespoons hot chili sauce
- 1 tablespoon mirin
- 25g ginger, finely grated
- Eight spring onions, cut into long pieces
- 500g leg steaks or pork loin, cut into thin strips
- cooked rice to serve

## INSTRUCTIONS

1. Mix 1 tablespoon of oil, the sesame seeds, chili sauce, soy sauce, ginger, and mirin. Pour over the pork and mix it all. Heat the remaining oil in a wok. Add the pork and fry for five minutes until browned. Add the spring onions and pepper and cook for five to ten minutes more until the vegetables have softened and the pork is cooked. Serve with cooked rice.

**NUTRITION: per serving**

• Protein: 39g • Fat: 21g • Carbs: 13g • Kcal: 407 • Sugars: 12g • Saturates: 4g • Fibre: 4g • Salt: 1.8g

## 7. TORNADO OMELETTE

Take eggs to a new level with a Korean-inspired 'tornado' omelette. It involves twirling chopsticks in the eggs to shape them as they cook in a hot pan.

| PREP TIME | COOK TIME | TOTAL TIME | SERVINGS |
|---|---|---|---|
| 5 Minutes | 5 Minutes | 10 Minutes | 1 |

## INGREDIENTS

- 1 teaspoon double cream
- One large egg
- toasted muffin and watercress (optional) to serve
- 1 teaspoon sunflower oil

## INSTRUCTIONS

1. Beat the cream and egg until fully mixed, then season with pepper and salt. Heat the oil in a small non-stick wok or omelet pan over medium heat. Pour the egg mix and wait thirty seconds for the bottom to set.
2. Working quickly, hold 2 chopsticks steady in the center of the omelet, then use the pan handle to turn the pan with the other hand, twisting the omelet into a tornado shape. Leave for thirty secs more to set (the top is meant to be runny), then ease out the chopsticks. Add more pepper, remove the omelet from the wok and place it on a toasted muffin with some watercress (optional).

**NUTRITION: Per serving**

• Protein: 8g • Fat: 13g • Kcal: 151 • Saturates: 5g • Fibre: 0g • Carbs: 0g • Sugars: 0g • Salt: 0.3g

## 8. BULGOGI

Marinate sliced beef in a classic Korean marinade, then pan-fry for a balance of sweet and savory flavors.

| PREP TIME | COOK TIME | TOTAL TIME | SERVINGS |
|-----------|-----------|------------|----------|
| 15 Minutes | 20 Minutes | 35 Minutes | 2 |

## INGREDIENTS

- 3 tablespoons dark brown sugar
- 1 ½ tablespoon roasted crushed sesame seeds
- 450g thinly sliced beef bulgogi meat (sold at Asian supermarkets), or sirloin
- One small unpeeled, firm but ripe pear, grated (optional)
- 2 tablespoons vegetable oil
- Five garlic cloves, crushed or grated
- 1 tablespoon toasted sesame seeds
- 3 tablespoons soy sauce
- 1 ½ tablespoon toasted sesame oil
- 1 ½ teaspoon grated ginger
- Four chives, snipped
- One small onion, thinly sliced
- One small carrot, julienned or chopped into fine matchsticks (see tip)
- Four white button mushrooms, sliced
- 1 tablespoon black sesame seeds

## INSTRUCTIONS

1. Mix the beef, pear and sugar thoroughly in a shallow dish, and leave to sit for thirty minutes at room temperature. In the meantime, in a large bowl, combine the soy sauce, 1 tablespoon of vegetable oil, sesame oil, garlic, sesame seeds, and ginger to make a marinade, and set aside.
2. When the beef is done, squeeze out any extra sugary liquid before adding it to the marinade. Toss to coat, cover and marinate at room temperature for thirty minutes. Can be marinated for longer or left in the fridge overnight.
3. The remaining vegetable oil should be heated over medium heat in a wok. Add the onion and cook for seven minutes until softened. Add the carrots and mushrooms and cook for five minutes until slightly softened. Increase the heat to medium-high, add the beef and marinade, and cook for five minutes, stirring periodically until the meat is browned. Place on a plate and top with sesame seeds and chives.

**Nutrition: per serving**

• Protein: 51g  • Fat: 36g  • Saturates: 9g  • Kcal: 694  • Carbs: 39g  • Fibre: 3g  • Sugars: 36g  • Salt: 4.4g

## 9. BEAN & HALLOUMI STEW

Make this halloumi-topped vegetable stew with tomatoes using a can of mixed beans. It takes only 25 minutes to prepare, making it the ideal midweek supper.

| PREP TIME | COOK TIME | TOTAL TIME | SERVINGS |
|-----------|-----------|------------|----------|
| 5 Minutes | 20 Minutes | 25 Minutes | 2 |

## INGREDIENTS

- One onion, thinly sliced
- 3 tablespoons olive oil
- One red pepper, thinly sliced
- 3 tablespoons red chili pesto, sundried tomato pesto or vegan alternative
- Two garlic cloves crushed
- 1 heaped teaspoon ground coriander
- 400g can chopped tomatoes
- 400g can mixed beans, drained, rinsed
- ½ x 250g block halloumi, sliced
- garlic bread, to serve (optional)
- ½ small bunch of coriander, finely chopped

## INSTRUCTIONS

1. Heat two tablespoons of oil in a wok over medium heat. Add the pepper and onion with a pinch of salt, and fry for ten minutes or until softened. Add the pesto, ground coriander, and garlic, and cook for one minute. Tip in the tomatoes and beans with ½ can of water, bring to a simmer, then cook uncovered for ten minutes.
2. Add the remaining oil to a separate frying pan over medium heat. Halloumi should be fried for two minutes on each side or until light brown.
3. Taste the beans for seasoning, and spoon into deep bowls. Top with the halloumi and scatter the chopped coriander on top. Serve with garlic bread (optional).

**Nutrition: Per serving**

• Kcal: 468 • Saturates: 7g • Fat: 25g • Carbs: 36g • Protein: 19g • Sugars: 12g • Fibre: 14g • Salt: 1.9g

# 10. LIVER AND ONIONS

A nostalgic thrifty dish, rich and nutritious. Serve the gravy drizzled over fluffy mashed potato

| PREP TIME | COOK TIME | TOTAL TIME | SERVINGS |
|---|---|---|---|
| 10 Minutes | 20 Minutes | 30 Minutes | 2 |

## INGREDIENTS

- 2 tablespoons plain flour, seasoned
- Four rashers smoked streaky bacon
- pinch dried sage (optional)
- 2 tablespoons ketchup
- 1 tablespoon olive oil
- 1 onion, thinly sliced
- 6 slices lamb's livers (about 400g/14oz)
- 300ml beef stock

## INSTRUCTIONS

1. Cook the bacon in a large non-stick wok until crisp. Meanwhile, mix the sage and flour, and use to dust the liver. Remove bacon from the wok and set aside. Add the oil to the wok and brown the liver for one minute on each side. Remove from the wok, fry the onion until tender. Stir in stock and ketchup, bubble for five minutes.
2. Return the liver to the wok and cook for three minutes until cooked. Serve with the bacon broken over the top and some mash.

### NUTRITION: per serving

• Kcal: 504  • Fibre: 3g  • Saturates: 7g  • Fat: 23g  • Carbs: 23g  • Protein: 53g  • Sugars: 7g  • Salt: 2.5g

# 11. CREAMY SALMON, LEEK & POTATO TRAYBAKE

| PREP TIME | COOK TIME | TOTAL TIME | SERVINGS |
|---|---|---|---|
| 5 Minutes | 35 Minutes | 40 Minutes | 2 |

Nestle leeks, potato and capers around salmon fillets to make this easy traybake for two. It's great as a midweek meal, or for a more romantic occasion

## INGREDIENTS

- 2 tablespoons olive oil
- 250g baby potatoes, thickly sliced
- One leek, halved, washed, sliced
- 70ml double cream
- One garlic clove, crushed
- 1 tablespoon capers, plus extra to serve
- 1 tablespoon chives, plus extra to serve
- mixed rocket salad, to serve (optional)
- Two skinless salmon fillets

## INSTRUCTIONS

1. Heat the oven to 180C fan/200C/gas 6. Bring a medium pan of water to a boil. Add the potatoes, then cook for eight minutes. Drain and leave to steam-dry in a colander for some minutes. Toss the potatoes with ½ of the oil and plenty of seasoning in a baking tray. Place in the oven for twenty minutes, tossing halfway through the cooking period.
2. In the meantime, heat the leftover oil in a wok over medium heat. Leeks should be added and fried for 5 minutes or until they start to tender. Stir through the garlic for one minute; add the capers, cream, capers, and 75ml hot water, then boil. Stir through the chives.
3. Heat the grill to high. Pour the creamy leek mixt over the potatoes, then sit the salmon fillets on top. Grill for eight minutes or until cooked. If desired, serve with a side salad and extra chives and capers on top.

**Nutrition: Per serving**

• Kcal: 714  • Saturates: 17g  • Fat: 52g  • Carbs: 20g  • Protein: 39g  • Sugars: 4g  • Fibre: 5g  • Salt: 0.5g

## 12. TOFU SCRAMBLE

Try our seasoned vegan tofu with cherry tomatoes for an egg-free take on a scramble on toast. Served on rye bread, ideal for breakfast.

| PREP TIME | COOK TIME | TOTAL TIME | SERVINGS |
|---|---|---|---|
| 10 Minutes | 20 Minutes | 30 Minutes | 2 |

## INGREDIENTS

- One small onion, finely sliced
- 1 tablespoon olive oil
- One large garlic clove, crushed
- 1 teaspoon ground cumin

- ½ teaspoon turmeric
- rye bread, to serve, (optional)
- ½ teaspoon sweet smoked paprika
- 100g cherry tomatoes, halved
- 280g extra firm tofu
- ½ small bunch of parsley, chopped

## INSTRUCTIONS

Heat the oil in a frying pan over medium heat and gently fry the onion for 8 -10 mins or until golden brown and sticky. Stir in the garlic, turmeric, cumin, and paprika and cook for 1 min.

Roughly mash the tofu in a bowl using a fork, keeping some pieces chunky. Add to the pan and fry for 3 mins. Raise the heat, then tip in the tomatoes, cooking for 5 mins more or until they soften. Fold the parsley through the mixture. Serve independently or with toasted rye bread (not gluten-free).

**Nutrition: Per serving**

• Kcal: 225  • Protein: 15g  • Saturates: 1.3g  • Fat: 14g  • Carbs: 7g  • Fibre: 3g  • Sugars: 4g  • Salt: 0.1g

## 13. BEST-EVER GAZPACHO

| PREP TIME | COOK TIME | TOTAL TIME | SERVINGS |
|-----------|-----------|------------|----------|
| 15 Minutes | 10 Minutes | 25 Minutes | 3 |

## INGREDIENTS

- Two Persian cucumbers, peeled, chopped
- 2 lb. tomatoes, quartered
- 1/2 red bell pepper, chopped
- 2 tablespoons sherry vinegar or red wine vinegar
- One clove garlic, roughly chopped
- 1/2 c. water
- Kosher salt
- 1/3 c. extra-virgin olive oil, plus more for garnish and pan
- Freshly ground black pepper
- 2 tablespoons of thinly sliced basil
- Two slices of country bread, cubed

## INSTRUCTIONS

1. Combine tomatoes, pepper, cucumbers, garlic, water, and vinegar in the bowl of a blender or food processor. Blend until smooth; add oil and blend to mix. Taste and season with pepper, salt, and more vinegar if needed. Cover and refrigerate until chilled.

2. In the meantime, heat enough oil in a large skillet or wok over medium heat, and add enough oil to coat the bottom of the pan. Add bread and cook, stirring periodically, until crisp and golden. Remove from heat, season with salt, and let cool.

3. Divide soup among plates and garnish with basil, croutons, and a drizzle of oil. Enjoy.

**NUTRITION: Per Serving (Serves 3)**

• Calories: 341 • Saturated fat: 4 g • Fat: 25 g • Trans-fat: 0 g • Sodium: 1114 mg • Carbohydrates: 20 g • Cholesterol: 0 mg • Fiber: 6 g • Vitamin D: 0 mcg • Iron 2: mg • Calcium: 81 mg • Sugar: 11 g • Protein: 6 g • Potassium: 914 mg

## 14. CHICKEN NOODLE SOUP

This broth will keep you warm on a chilly winter evening - it includes ginger, which is good for colds.

| PREP TIME | COOK TIME | TOTAL TIME | SERVINGS |
|-----------|-----------|------------|----------|
| 10 Minutes | 30 Minutes | 40 Minutes | 2 |

## INGREDIENTS

- One boneless, skinless chicken breast (about 175g)
- 900ml chicken or Miso soup mix or vegetable stock
- 1 teaspoon chopped fresh ginger
- 50g wheat noodles or rice
- One garlic clove, finely chopped
- 2 tablespoons sweetcorn, canned or frozen
- 2 spring onions, shredded
- 2-3 mushrooms, thinly sliced
- Basil or mint leaves and a little shredded chili to serve (optional)
- 2 teaspoons soy sauce, plus extra for serving

## INSTRUCTIONS

1. Pour the stock into a pan, and add the chicken breast, garlic, and ginger. Once it has boiled, turn the heat down, partly cover, and cook the chicken for 20 minutes or until it is soft.

2. Put the chicken on a board, then shred the chicken into bite-sized chunks using a couple of forks. Return the chicken to the stock with the sweetcorn, mushrooms, noodles, soy sauce, and spring onion. Simmer for four minutes until the noodles are tender.

3. If using, ladle into 2 bowls and scatter the remaining basil or mint leaves, spring onion, and chili. Serve with extra soy sauce.

**NUTRITION: per serving**

• Kcal: 217 • Protein: 26g • Saturates: 0.4g • Fat: 2g • Carbs: 26g • Fibre: 0.6g • Sugars: 1g • Salt: 2.5g

# 15. KOREAN FRIED CHICKEN

Make these hot and sticky Korean chicken wings for a delicious yet simple dinner. They make the perfect finger food, but do not forget the napkins.

| PREP TIME | COOK TIME | TOTAL TIME | SERVINGS |
|---|---|---|---|
| 15 Minutes | 15 Minutes | 30 Minutes | 4 |

## INGREDIENTS

### For the chicken

- sliced spring onion and sesame seeds, to serve
- large chunk of ginger, finely grated
- 500g chicken wings
- vegetable oil, for frying
- 50g corn flour

### For the sauce

- 2 teaspoons sesame oil
- 2 tablespoons gochujang (Korean chili paste)
- 6 tablespoons dark brown sugar
- 2 tablespoons soy sauce
- small piece of ginger, grated
- Two large garlic cloves, crushed

## INSTRUCTIONS

1. Put all the ingredients in a saucepan and gently simmer for 3–4 minutes or until syrupy. Remove from the heat and set aside.
2. Season the chicken wings with pepper, grated ginger, and salt. Toss the chicken with the cornflour until fully coated.
3. Heat about 2cm of vegetable oil in a large frying pan over medium/high heat. Chicken wings should be fried for 8 to 10 minutes, turning them halfway through. Remove from the oil and place on kitchen paper. Allow to cool (around 2 minutes).
4. Reheat the sauce and toss the crispy chicken wings in it. Put in a dish and garnish with sliced spring onion and sesame seeds.

**Nutrition: per serving**

• Kcal: 487  • Protein: 20g  • Saturates: 4g  • Fat: 24g  • Carbs: 48g  • Fibre: 1g  • Sugars: 35g  • Salt: 1.8g

## 16. KOREAN-STYLE FRIED RICE

This quick Korean recipe is extremely satisfying and a fantastic way to use up extra cooked rice. It also full of iron.

| PREP TIME | COOK TIME | TOTAL TIME | SERVINGS |
|---|---|---|---|
| 10 Minutes | 15 Minutes | 25 Minutes | 4 |

## INGREDIENTS

- 350g rump steak
- 3 tablespoons sesame oil
- 250g mushrooms (we used chestnut), sliced
- 2 tablespoons soy sauce
- Three garlic cloves, thinly sliced
- 1 tablespoon chili sauce (we used sriracha), plus extra to serve
- 200g beansprouts
- 500g cooked rice (200g/7oz uncooked)
- Four eggs
- bunch spring onions, sliced

## INSTRUCTIONS

1. Heat 1 tablespoon of the oil in a frying pan or a wok over high heat, season the steaks, then cook for two to three minutes on each side. Take out of the wok and set aside to rest.
2. Heat 1 tablespoon oil in a separate frying pan, stir-fry the mushrooms until softened, and stir in the beansprouts, soy, chili sauce, and garlic. Cook for two more minutes, then add the cooked rice and heat through. Stir in the spring onions and keep warm.
3. Heat the remaining oil in the pan or wok in which you fried the steak. Add the eggs and fry until done. Slice the steaks and spoon the rice into bowls. Top each one with an egg, the sliced steak, and a drizzle of chili sauce.

**NUTRITION: per serving**

• Kcal: 530  • Protein: 38g  • Saturates: 7g  • Fat: 25g  • Crbs: 41g  • Fibre: 3g  • Sugars: 3g  • Salt: 1.9g

# 17. KOREAN FISHCAKES WITH FRIED EGGS & SPICY SALSA

| PREP TIME | COOK TIME | TOTAL TIME | SERVINGS |
|-----------|-----------|------------|----------|
| 15 Minutes | 12 Minutes | 27 Minutes | 4 |

This isn't your average fishcake recipe. Bursting with oriental flavors - soy sauce, fresh ginger, spring onions, and gochujang, topped with a rich, runny yolk - this recipe has it all

## INGREDIENTS

### For the fishcakes

- 2 teaspoons finely grated ginger
- One large egg white, beaten until frothy
- 4 x rainbow trout or loch trout fillets, skinned, cut into 1cm/ 1/2in pieces (about 1lb/450g fish)
- One fat garlic clove, crushed
- bunch spring onions, thinly sliced
- 1 teaspoon light soy sauce
- 2 ½ tablespoons vegetable oil for frying
- 2 tablespoons rice flour

### For the salad

- 100g radishes, thinly sliced
- One pointed or small white cabbage, cored, finely shredded (about 350g/12oz)
- 2 tablespoons Chinese rice vinegar
- One red chili, finely sliced, to serve (optional)
- 1 teaspoon gochujang, plus two top to serve
- 1 tablespoon sesame oil, plus 2 teaspoons to serve
- 1 teaspoon golden caster sugar
- Four medium eggs
- One garlic clove, crushed
- 2 teaspoons light soy sauce
- 1 tablespoon sesame seeds, toasted

## INSTRUCTIONS

1. Combine the fish with the ginger, soy, garlic, and half the spring onions to make the fishcakes. Stir in the rice flour and egg white.
2. Toss the radishes and cabbage with vinegar, 1 tablespoon sesame oil, 1 teaspoon gochujang, and the garlic and sugar. Set aside. Stir together the remaining sesame oil, the soy sauce, and the gochujang to make a drizzling sauce for later.
3. Heat 1 tablespoon oil in a large, non-stick wok. Divide the fish mixture into eight equal portions, then spoon four into the wok and press the mixture to form cakes about 8cm across. Fry for 2 minutes on each side or

until cooked and golden. Add another 1 tablespoon of oil to the pan, and repeat with the remaining fish. Keep warm in a low oven.

4. Add the remaining oil to the pan. Fry the eggs for two minutes until crisp but with a runny yolk. Serve the fishcakes with the cabbage, and top with the sesame seeds and egg. Scatter with the remaining spring onions, red chili, and some of the chili sesame drizzle

**NUTRITION: per serving**

• Kcal: 451  • Protein: 35g  • Saturates: 4g  • Fat: 27g  • Carbs: 15g  • Fibre: 4g  • Sugars: 7g  • Salt: 1g

## 18. CELERY SOUP

| PREP TIME | COOK TIME | TOTAL TIME | SERVINGS |
|-----------|-----------|------------|----------|
| 15 Minutes | 40 Minutes | 55 Minutes | 3-4 |

Cook up a batch of fresh, low-calorie celery soup for a healthy and filling veggie lunch or supper. Serve with chunks of crusty bread

## INGREDIENTS

- 300g celery, sliced, with tough strings removed
- 2 tablespoons olive oil
- crusty bread to serve
- One garlic clove, peeled
- 500ml vegetable stock
- 200g potatoes, peeled, cut into chunks
- 100ml milk

## INSTRUCTIONS

1. Heat the oil in a large wok over medium heat. Tip in the garlic, celery, and potatoes, and coat in the oil. Add a splash of water and a pinch of salt and cook, stirring for fifteen minutes, adding a little more water if the veg begins to stick.
2. Pour in the vegetable stock and boil, then turn the heat down and simmer for twenty more minutes until the celery is soft and the potatoes are falling apart. Use a stick blender to purée the soup, then pour in the milk and blitz again. Season to taste. Serve with crusty bread.

**Nutrition: per serving (3)**

• Protein: 3g  • Kcal: 163  • Saturates: 2g  • Fat: 9g  • Carbs: 15g  • Fibre: 3g  • Sugars: 4g  • Salt: 0.6g

## 19. MUSHROOM STROGANOFF

| PREP TIME | COOK TIME | TOTAL TIME | SERVINGS |
|-----------|-----------|------------|----------|
| 10 Minutes | 20 Minutes | 30 Minutes | 2 |

A few clever substitutions can make this traditional creamy casserole low in fat and calories

## INGREDIENTS

- One onion, finely chopped
- 2 teaspoons olive oil
- 250g pouch cooked wild rice
- 1 tablespoon sweet paprika
- 300g mixed mushrooms, chopped
- Two garlic cloves crushed
- 150ml low-sodium beef or vegetable stock
- 3 tablespoons half-fat soured cream
- 1 tablespoon Worcestershire sauce or vegetarian alternative
- small bunch of parsley, roughly chopped

## INSTRUCTIONS

1. Heat the olive oil in a large non-stick wok and soften the onion for five minutes.
2. Stir in the garlic and paprika, and simmer for an additional minute. Add the mushrooms and cook for five minutes on high heat, stirring often.
3. Pour in the stock and Worcestershire sauce. Bring to a boil, bubble for five minutes until the sauce thickens, turn off the heat, and stir through the soured cream and most of the parsley. Ensure the wok isn't on the heat or the sauce may split.
4. Heat the wild rice following pack instructions and stir through the remaining chopped parsley. Serve with stroganoff.

**NUTRITION: per serving**

• Kcal: 329  • Protein: 11g  • Saturates: 1g  • Fat: 9g  • Carbs: 50g  • Fibre: 4g  • Sugars: 8g  • Salt: 0.7g

## 20. KOREAN FRIED RICE

| PREP TIME | COOK TIME | TOTAL TIME | SERVINGS |
|---|---|---|---|
| 10 Minutes | 20-25 Minutes | 30-35 Minutes | 4 |

Looking for a simple rice dish with a bit of spice? Our Korean fried rice has beautifully seasoned steak strips and shredded cabbage for extra crunch

## INGREDIENTS

- 2 x frying steaks (approx 7oz/200g), sliced into strips
- 2 tablespoons sesame seeds
- 250g white basmati rice
- 3 tablespoons chili sauce (such as sriracha), plus extra to serve
- Two garlic cloves, finely sliced
- 2 tablespoons sesame oil
- Six spring onions, finely sliced
- ½ large Savoy cabbage, shredded
- 1-2 red chilies, finely sliced

## INSTRUCTIONS

1. Cook the rice following pack instructions. Meanwhile, mix the steak strips with the chili sauce in a bowl to marinate.
2. Heat 1 tablespoon of the oil in a wok over high heat and stir-fry the meat for two minutes until beginning to color.
3. Now, resist the urge to overcook the steak because you still want it slightly pink in the center. Once done, set it aside on a plate.
4. Add most of the spring onions and chilies, and garlic to the wok, reserving some to serve, and keep stir-frying for two minutes. Add the cabbage, then cook gently for ten minutes until beginning to soften.
5. Bring the rice and steak back to the wok and stir everything together thoroughly. Sprinkle over the sesame seeds, the reserved chilies, and spring onions, and drizzle over more chili sauce to serve.

**NUTRITION: per serving**

• Kcal: 510  • Protein: 28g  • Fat: 19g  • Carbs: 56g  • Fibre: 4g  • Saturates: 6g  • Sugars: 5g  • Salt: 0.7g

**IMAGES Reference:**

www.bbcgoodfood.com andlervid85 on Freepik 2008 EyesWideOpen
Image by https://www.freepik.com/free-photo/high-angle-vegetables-getting-sauteed-pan_32201720.htm#query=wok%20cooking&position=28&from_view=search&track=robertav1
Freepik imago images/R Modi/Dinodia Photo